O9-AIG-057

Writing the Critical Essay

Universal Health Care

An OPPOSING VIEWPOINTS® Guide

Lauri S. Friedman, *Book Editor*

OPPOSING VIEWPOINTS® SERIES

GREENHAVEN PRESS
A part of Gale, Cengage Learning

GALE
CENGAGE Learning™

Detroit • New York • San Francisco • New Haven, Conn • Waterville, Maine • London

GALE
CENGAGE Learning

Christine Nasso, *Publisher*
Elizabeth Des Chenes, *Managing Editor*

Articles in Greenhaven Press anthologies are often edited for length to meet page requirements. In addition, original titles of these works are changed to clearly present the main thesis and to explicitly indicate the author's opinion. Every effort is made to ensure that Greenhaven Press accurately reflects the original intent of the authors. Every effort has been made to trace the owners of copyrighted material.

Cover image © Jim West/Alamy.

LIBRARY OF CONGRESS CATALOGING-IN-PUBLICATION DATA

Universal health care / Lauri S. Friedman, book editor.
    p. cm. -- (Writing the critical essay : an opposing viewpoints guide)
 Includes bibliographical references and index.
 ISBN 978-0-7377-5539-8 (hardcover)
 1. Health care reform--United States. 2. Right to health care. I. Friedman, Lauri S.
 RA395.A3U587 2011
 362.1'0425--dc22
                                                                    2011003585

3 1907 00287 8204

Printed in the United States of America
1 2 3 4 5 6 7 15 14 13 12 11

CONTENTS

Examining the state of writing and how it is taught in the United States was the official purpose of the National Commission on Writing in America's Schools and Colleges. The commission, made up of teachers, school administrators, business leaders, and college and university presidents, released its first report in 2003. "Despite the best efforts of many educators," commissioners argued, "writing has not received the full attention it deserves." Among the findings of the commission was that most fourth-grade students spent less than three hours a week writing, that three-quarters of high school seniors never receive a writing assignment in their history or social studies classes, and that more than 50 percent of first-year students in college have problems writing error-free papers. The commission called for a "cultural sea change" that would increase the emphasis on writing for both elementary and secondary schools. These conclusions have made some educators realize that writing must be emphasized in the curriculum. As colleges are demanding an ever-higher level of writing proficiency from incoming students, schools must respond by making students more competent writers. In response to these concerns, the SAT, an influential standardized test used for college admissions, required an essay for the first time in 2005.

Books in the Writing the Critical Essay: An Opposing Viewpoints Guide series use the patented Opposing Viewpoints format to help students learn to organize ideas and arguments and to write essays using common critical writing techniques. Each book in the series focuses on a particular type of essay writing—including expository, persuasive, descriptive, and narrative—that students learn while being taught both the five-paragraph essay as well as longer pieces of writing that have an opinionated focus. These guides include everything necessary to help students research, outline, draft, edit, and ultimately write successful essays across the curriculum, including essays for the SAT.

Using Opposing Viewpoints

This series is inspired by and builds upon Greenhaven Press's acclaimed Opposing Viewpoints series. As in the parent series, each book in the Writing the Critical Essay series focuses on a timely and controversial social issue that provides lots of opportunities for creating thought-provoking essays. The first section of each volume begins with a brief introductory essay that provides context for the opposing viewpoints that follow. These articles are chosen for their accessibility and clearly stated views. The thesis of each article is made explicit in the article's title and is accentuated by its pairing with an opposing or alternative view. These essays are both models of persuasive writing techniques and valuable research material that students can mine to write their own informed essays. Guided reading and discussion questions help lead students to key ideas and writing techniques presented in the selections.

The second section of each book begins with a preface discussing the format of the essays and examining characteristics of the featured essay type. Model five-paragraph and longer essays then demonstrate that essay type. The essays are annotated so that key writing elements and techniques are pointed out to the student. Sequential, step-by-step exercises help students construct and refine thesis statements; organize material into outlines; analyze and try out writing techniques; write transitions, introductions, and conclusions; and incorporate quotations and other researched material. Ultimately, students construct their own compositions using the designated essay type.

The third section of each volume provides additional research material and writing prompts to help the student. Additional facts about the topic of the book serve as a convenient source of supporting material for essays. Other features help students go beyond the book for their research. Like other Greenhaven Press books, each book in the Writing the Critical Essay series includes bibliographic listings of relevant periodical articles, books, Web sites, and organizations to contact.

Writing the Critical Essay: An Opposing Viewpoints Guide will help students master essay techniques that can be used in any discipline.

The 2010 Patient Protection and Affordable Care Act

In March 2010, Congress and President Barack Obama passed the Patient Protection and Affordable Care Act (PPACA), which reformed health care in the United States. Nicknamed "Obamacare" after the president who made health care reform a key piece of his election campaign and championed it once in office, the PPACA was nothing short of historic. Previous reforms had expanded health care for the poor (via Medicaid, established by the Social Security Act in 1965), the elderly (via Medicare, also established by the Social Security Act), and for children (via the State Children's Health Insurance Program, or SCHIP, in 1997). But the PPACA was the first attempt to reform health care for all sectors of the population.

The PPACA is vast, but features several core and key provisions. Among them are laws designed to protect Americans from being exploited by insurance companies or denied coverage entirely. To this end, the PPACA prohibits health plans from rejecting people who have prior health issues, otherwise known as "preexisting conditions." It also makes it illegal for health insurance companies to charge customers higher premiums because of their gender or current health status. In addition, insurance companies will not be allowed to drop most customers from their plans if and when they get sick, nor will they be allowed to place a ceiling on the amount or extent to which a sick person can access coverage.

The PPACA also offers tax credits to small businesses that offer their employees health insurance. It requires most individuals to have health insurance as of 2014, but will help some of them pay for the coverage, and removes obstacles that previously kept them from being insurable.

It increases funding for community health centers, provides funds to increase the number of practicing doctors, nurses, nurse practitioners, and physician assistants and has numerous other features. Some parts of the law were effective as of 2011; others do not take effect until 2012, 2013, or even 2014.

Getting the PPACA passed was a monumental legislative effort that took Congress nearly a year to accomplish. Yet after all the compromising, negotiating, and haggling, most Americans were displeased with what the government came up with. A December 2010 ABC News/*Washington Post* poll found that just 43 percent of Americans strongly or somewhat supported the final health care reform law: 51 percent strongly or somewhat opposed it. The greatest evidence of the public's dissatisfaction with the law was that even before most of it even took effect, there was talk of repealing it: A November 2010 Quinnipiac University poll found 47 percent of Americans thought the 2010 health care law should be repealed, while 30 percent wanted to see it changed in some way. Only 18 percent thought it should be left as is.

The law's final form clearly pleased very few Americans. But interestingly, those disappointed in it were upset for vastly different reasons. Conservatives complained that the law went too far; liberals, that it did not go far enough.

Conservatives cited several reasons why they opposed passage of the law. Among them was its price. They claimed that the law's cost—$940 billion over the course of a decade—was simply too much to bear for a nation struggling through a tough recession. They charged that health care reform would add to the nation's already staggering deficit. In addition to cost, conservatives opposed the law for ideological reasons, too. They argued the law would inappropriately add to the government's power; they also disagreed with the law's premise that access to health care is a human right. Given these complaints, not a single Republican senator or representative voted for it. Moreover, Republicans were particularly incensed by the law's passage: 86 percent of them described the law as "bad for the country" in an October 2010 *Newsweek* poll, while 85 percent of them told the Quinnipiac University researchers that the act should be repealed.

While conservatives denounced the PPACA for its cost and scope, their liberal counterparts were displeased with the law for the opposite reason: they claimed that the law did not go far enough. Indeed, the November 2010 Quinnipiac University poll found that 30 percent of the general public thought the PPACA should be expanded, and 53 percent of Democrats thought this. Specifically, Democrats were disappointed that a government-run health insurance option was not included in the act. Known as a "public option," such a plan would have created a government-run health insurance plan that could have offered Americans an alternative to private insurance companies. A 2009 poll conducted by CBS News found high support for a public option: 61 percent of Americans said that they supported including such an option in the health care reform bill. Support was massive among Democrats: 82 percent favored its inclusion. To their dismay, in December 2009 the public option that had passed through the House of Representatives was dropped from the final text of the bill in a compromise effort to get some form of health care reform passed through the Senate.

In addition to widespread disappointment among both Republicans and Democrats, since the PPACA's passage, eighteen states have sued the federal government over the bill, and in December 2010 a Virginia judge launched the first of what are likely to be numerous legal challenges to the law's constitutionality. Yet the law's most ardent supporter implored his fellow citizens to have patience with the process and give the government time to build upon these initial accomplishments. "We have passed historic healthcare reform," Barack Obama told *Daily Show* host Jon Stewart in October 2010. "We have moved forward an agenda that is making a difference in people's lives each and every day. Now, is it enough? No . . . [but] my expectation and hope is, if you look at the track record that we've accomplished in very difficult circumstances over the last 18 months, we have done an awful lot . . . and we're gonna do more in the years to come."[1] Many agreed with the president and pointed out that several of the nation's signature programs took decades to develop. "Just as Social Security grew from a modest start in 1935 to become a bedrock of the nation's retirement system," wrote the *New York Times* editorial board upon the passage of the PPACA, "this is a start on health care reform, not the end."[2]

Whether the 2010 health care law went too far, not far enough, or struck the right balance is one of the many issues explored in *Writing the Critical Essay: Universal Health Care.* Cogently argued viewpoints and model essays explore whether health care is a fundamental human right, whether providing universal health care is too expensive, and whether it will improve the quality of medical care. Thought-provoking writing exercises and step-by-step instructions help readers write their own five-paragraph persuasive essays on this complicated and timely subject.

Notes

1. Barack Obama, interviewed by Jon Stewart, *The Daily Show*, October 27, 2010. www.thedailyshow.com/ watch/wed-october-27-2010/barack-obama-pt--1.
2. "Health Care Reform, at Last," *New York Times*, March 21, 2010. www.nytimes.com/2010/03/22/opinion/ 22mon5.html?pagewanted = all.

Section One:
Opposing
Viewpoints
on Universal
Health Care

Medicare

Health Care Is a Fundamental Human Right

Bryan Young

In the following essay, Bryan Young argues that health care is a basic human right. He explains that as a self-employed person, he does not have health insurance through an employer. This means he has to pay for care at full price, which is outrageously expensive. Young describes the agony of feeling forced to choose between getting the care one needs and going into debt for tens of thousands of dollars. He says no one should have to forgo care because one cannot afford it. In his opinion, the just, humane, and Christian thing to do is make sure sick, suffering people can access medical care without bankrupting themselves to do it.

Bryan Young is a filmmaker and writer.

Consider the following questions:

1. What two thoughts does Young say cross his mind when a medical emergency strikes?
2. How much did it cost to treat the author's son's burns?
3. What, according to Young, should Americans be ashamed of?

I draw a modest income with my media production business, but being self-employed makes health insurance damn near impossible to afford. Hell, with the way self-employment taxes are set up, we're lucky to be able to pay those.

Bryan Young, "A Good Case for Universal Health Care," HuffingtonPost.com, June 7, 2008. Reproduced by permission of the author.

Because of this catch-22 [no-win situation] (running your own business at the expense of normal company perks like medical care), I find myself thinking things that no one in an emergency should have to deal with. You see, at a Mother's Day barbecue last month [May 2008], my son accidentally lit himself on fire. The barbecue was luau themed and he was wearing a grass skirt. Getting too close to an open flame with all of that dead grass and he was quickly running in circles in the backyard trying to put himself out before family members came to his aid.

"How Will I Pay For It?"
My first thought (other than, "Jesus, he's on fire!") was, "Is this bad enough to need an emergency room visit?"

Demonstrators march to encourage health care reform. Many believe health care is a fundamental human right.

As soon as I got close enough to see that the skin on his hands and legs was bubbled over and charred, I realized that it was, indeed, bad enough to need a visit.

My second thought was, "But how will I pay for it?"

It's sad and disgusting to me that these things were forced to enter my mind when my only thought should have been getting my son immediately to the hospital. Fortunately, these questions were but split seconds in my judgment and we were in the car racing to the hospital in minutes.

The local emergency room didn't have the facilities to deal with burns as extensive and deep as my sons were, so we were quickly ambulanced to a facility at the University of Utah renowned for it's Burn Trauma Intensive Care Unit [ICU]. (40 mile ambulance ride? $2,000)

> ## Health Care Is Everyone's Right
>
> **Health care is everyone's right as surely as the right to breathe and the right to eat.**
>
> Henry J. Amoroso, "Health Care Is a Fundamental Right," *National Catholic Reporter*, September 29, 2009. http://ncronline.org/news/justice/health-care-fundamental-Right.

Balancing Cost with Care

When we got there, the doctors went to work, cutting his blisters off, treating his wounds and making assessments about the possibility of skin grafting. He had 2nd degree burns over 10% of his body and a few spots were on the border of 3rd degree. I spent 8 sleepless nights in that ICU with my son, helping clean his wounds and wash the dead skin and scabs off twice a day, knowing that this would all cost me more money than I could imagine. But I did it anyway, without regard to the cost because no matter how well off or poor, well insured or not insured at all, medical emergencies take precedence over monetary consideration.

We were able to bring him home just a couple of days before his birthday, though he still needed twice-a-day wound care (and still does). The total cost of this ordeal if I end up having to pay for it out of my own pocket? In excess of $25,000.

But did I have a choice?

No.

Forced to Writhe in Pain

But things got worse. The night we brought him home, the most improbable thing in the world happened. I was struck with severe abdominal pain. The worst I've ever had in my life.

Again, I started asking myself these questions (after, "Jesus, this hurts like hell!"), "Is it bad enough to need a trip to the emergency room?"

After the first hour, I thought I could self-medicate the pain away. I don't get heartburn, but I assumed this might be what it's like, so I decided antacids (which I've never used) might help.

Another hour of writhing in pain with no help from antacids went by and I had to reassess my situation, "This still hurts like hell, and the antacids didn't work. Do I go to the hospital?"

Knowing that I couldn't afford a trip to the hospital, I decided I'd try more self-medication. "Perhaps I've pulled a muscle, or inflamed something," I thought. And then I proceeded to take some Ibuprofen; hoping painkillers might dull the pain.

Yet another hour of painful torture went by and I was forced again to assess the situation, "It actually hurts worse now, antacids and painkillers didn't help at all, perhaps it's something serious. But can I afford a trip to the hospital?"

The answer I came to was that, even if something serious were wrong, I couldn't afford a trip to the hospital and so I decided that the best course of action was to try sleeping off the pain.

Unfortunately, this didn't work either. I spent two hours in bed, tossing and turning, trying my hardest to find a position comfortable enough to wait out the pain. No comfortable middle-ground could be found and after 6 hours of excruciating pain and the knowledge that I wouldn't be able to sleep, suddenly, the cost of a trip to the hospital didn't seem so consequential.

But why should anyone be forced to writhe in pain for fear of having to pay for a trip to the emergency room?

Teachers in McCracken County wore "Help Us Please" stickers to protest a proposed insurance plan. Those without insurance often find themselves avoiding needed care because they fear the medical bills.

Shouldn't we, as a society, make sure that when people are in pain, that they are able to seek treatment without the fear of eternal debt and foreclosure and anything else medicals bills of impressive size would cause?

Universal Healthcare Would Be Safer, Easier, and Cheaper

I went to the hospital and discovered that I had a severe case of gallstones and my gallbladder needed to be removed immediately to prevent worse problems, including death. I didn't really have a choice about this one. I prolonged my decision because of the economics of seeing a doctor and I could have made things a lot worse. The total cost of that operation? In excess of $15,000.

By the end of May, my son and I managed to incur more than $40,000 worth of medical debt. We're working on a couple of options to cover some or all of this (including Medicaid which is a paper-work nightmare but a dream come true if it works out).

But the point is this, I've actually spent more time filling out papers, answering questions, and tracking down documents and pay records trying to get help with these bills than I actually spent in the hospital.

How much safer, easier, cheaper and more pleasant would all of our lives be with single payer universal healthcare? To be able to breathe easy and see the doctor when you need to. To be able to have life-saving surgeries and not worry that you might have to sell your car or go late on your rent? Millions of Americans have problems like this every day and we should be ashamed of ourselves that we've led our culture so far down this road.

We Should Be Ashamed

As for me? I'll probably end up ok, it seems as though I can get help for my son's bills with a couple of different government programs (like Medicaid or SCHIP). The chances of me getting help with the bills for my surgery are a little lower, but in any case, I'm sure I'll weather the storm. But for every case like mine, I'm sure there are a dozen families who simply can't weather the storm, and for that, we should be ashamed.

I'm sure there are a dozen Christian conservatives reading this now and asking themselves, "Why should we help with this? Why should we help people who can't afford to take care of themselves?"

In the novel *Jailbird*, Kurt Vonnegut provided me with the perfect answer to these questions and it's very simple: "Why? The Sermon on the Mount, sir."

Analyze the essay:

1. Young says he would tell people opposed to universal health care to think of the Sermon on the Mount. Explain what he means by this and how it supports his argument.

2. To make his argument, Young offers two personal stories—his gallbladder operation and his son's burn incident. Did the use of these personal and true anecdotes compel you to agree with Young that health care is a basic human right? Why or why not?

Health Care Is Not a Fundamental Human Right

Jacob G. Hornberger

Jacob G. Hornberger is the founder and president of the Future of Freedom Foundation. In the following essay, he explains why he thinks health care is not a basic human right. Rights offered by the Declaration of Independence guarantee a person's freedom to pursue life, liberty, and happiness, he says. They do not guarantee a person will achieve these things, however. In his opinion, Americans are confused about the true meaning of rights. Hornberger says it is true that the government cannot interfere with a person's right to pursue health care. But he also says that the government is in no way obligated to provide health care, either. He reminds readers there is no such thing as "free" health care. Other Americans must foot the bill for those who do not pay. Hornberger concludes that health care—like food, clothing, and shelter—is something all citizens have the right to seek for themselves but not the right to receive for free.

Consider the following questions:

1. What does Hornberger say would essentially turn doctors into slaves?
2. Who is Bastiat and how does he factor into the author's argument?
3. What, according to Hornberger, is the true nature of rights?

Jacob G. Hornberger, "Health Care Is Not a Right," Future of Freedom Foundation, July 1, 2009. Reproduced by permission.

A midst all the health care debate, there is one underlying assumption that hardly anyone challenges: the notion that people have a right to health care. The truth is that it's a nonsensical notion. People no more have a right to health care than they have a right to education, food, or clothing.

Examining the Notion of a "Right" to Health Care

After all, what does a right to health care mean? If I have a right to something, then doesn't that mean that you have a correlative duty to provide it? If you're a doctor, then it means that you are required to serve my needs, like it or not. If I need an operation, then you cannot say "no" because that would be denying me my right to health care.

Thus, isn't the right to health care actually a power to force doctors to provide people with medical services?

Now, the proponent of health care as a right might say, "That's not what I mean. Why, to force doctors to provide health care services to others would be akin to slavery, especially if it's for free. I think that doctors deserve to be paid for their services."

Fair enough. But then doesn't the right to health care entail the power to force someone else to pay for it? Let's assume, for example, that I need hip-replacement surgery that will cost $25,000 and that I don't have the money to pay for it. Since I have a right to health care, that means that I have a right to get the money from you to pay for my operation. It also means that you can't say no because that would be interfering with my right to health care.

Health Care Is Not a Constitutional Right

Constitutional rights such as freedom of speech and religion and the right to property can be clearly defined in accordance with John Stuart Mill's harm principle—act as you will so long as you do not directly harm others. In contrast, the expansive "rights" demanded by liberals—like the right to "affordable health care" or to a 'decent standard of living'—are not rights but positive demands that require others to hand over some of the property to the claimant.

Iain Murray and Roger Abbott, "Health Care Is Not a Right," *Washington Examiner*, November 17, 2009. www.washingtonexaminer.com/opinion/blogs/ Examiner- Opinion-Zone/Health-Care-is-not-a-right-70302612.html.

Someone Has to Pay for Those Who Cannot

Thus, the right to health care entails the power of everyone to get into the pocketbooks of everyone else. That's not only a ridiculous notion of rights but also a highly destructive one. Since obviously people can't go and take the money from others directly, it inevitably entails converting government into an engine of seizure and redistribution. Or to paraphrase [French theorist Claude Frédéric] Bastiat, such a concept of rights converts government into a fiction by which everyone is doing his best to live at the expense of everyone else.

Meanwhile, while everyone is using government to get into everyone else's pocketbook to pay for his health care expenses, he is simultaneously doing his best to protect his own income and assets from being plundered by the government to fund everyone else's health care bills.

Over time, it is easy to see how such a system devolves into everyone's warring against everyone else. It is also easy to see that such a system obviously does not nurture friendly and harmonious relations between people. This is especially true when these types of "rights" expand to such areas as education, food, clothing, and housing.

Rights Are to Be Pursued, Not Granted

The true nature of rights—the type of rights the Founding Fathers believed in—involved the right of people to pursue such things as health care, education, clothing, and food and that government cannot legitimately interfere with their ability to do so.

Thus, the right to life, liberty, and the pursuit of happiness, as described in the Declaration of Independence, doesn't mean that someone else is forced to provide you with the means to sustain or improve your life. It means that government cannot enact laws, rules, or regulations that interfere with or infringe upon your right to pursue such things.

When Americans began looking upon rights as some sort of positive duty on others to provide them with

Jacob Hornberger argues that the "right" to health care simply means a doctor is required to serve a patient's needs.

certain things, that was when the quality of health care in America began plummeting. That was what Medicare and Medicaid were all about—the so-called right of poor people and the elderly to health care. It is not a coincidence that what began as the finest health care system in the world has turned into a system that is now in perpetual crisis.

Fixing the System Involves Abandoning the Idea of "Rights"

There is one—and only one—solution to America's health care woes—and it lies not in a government takeover of health care. In fact, the solution is the exact opposite: It is the end of all government involvement in health care—a

Americans Are Satisfied with Health Care as It Is

A 2009 poll found that most Americans are satisfied with the cost and quality of their health insurance and health care and see no need to radically change the system.

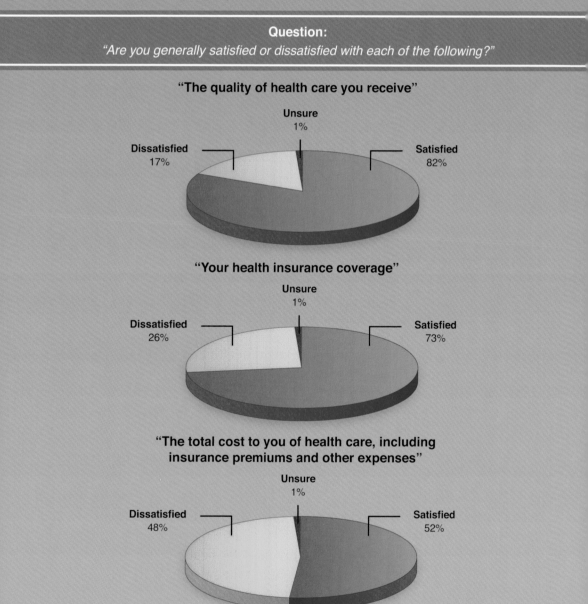

"The quality of health care you receive"

Unsure
1%

Dissatisfied
17%

Satisfied
82%

"Your health insurance coverage"

Unsure
1%

Dissatisfied
26%

Satisfied
73%

"The total cost to you of health care, including insurance premiums and other expenses"

Unsure
1%

Dissatisfied
48%

Satisfied
52%

Taken from: CNN/Opinion Research Corporation poll, March 12–15, 2009.

total separation of health care and the state. That would entail not a reform or improvement of Medicare and Medicaid but rather their total repeal.

At its core, the solution to America's health care crisis lies in the abandonment of the notion that health care is a right. Once people reach this fundamental realization, as our American ancestors did, the nation can get back on the road toward a healthy, prosperous, and harmonious society.

The rights given in the US Constitution and the Declaration of Independence are to be pursued, not automatically granted, according to those who oppose universal health care.

Universal Health Care Will Be Too Expensive

Larry Kudlow

In the following essay, Larry Kudlow argues that universal health care will bankrupt the nation. He says government programs are notoriously expensive and inefficient. In this tradition, he predicts a government-run health care program will cost trillions of dollars and not work very well. The nation cannot afford such a program given the fact it is already spending beyond its means, contends Kudlow. In addition to being expensive, public health care would put the government in the position of telling people which procedures, tests, and drugs they can or cannot have, Kudlow warns. In his opinion, this would threaten their freedom. For all of these reasons, he concludes that health care should remain a private industry that is regulated by the free market.

Larry Kudlow is an economist who writes columns for several publications, including the *National Review*.

Consider the following questions:

1. About how much additional money does Kudlow expect a public health care program would cost?
2. To whom does Kudlow say tax breaks for health care should go?
3. What two effects does Kudlow say free-market competition for health care would have?

Larry Kudlow, "Obama's 'Public' Health Plan Will Bankrupt the Nation," *National Review*, May 3, 2009. Reproduced by permission.

Does anybody really believe that adding 50 million people to the public health-care rolls will *not* cost the government more money? About $1.5 trillion to $2 trillion more? At least.

So let's be serious when evaluating President [Barack] Obama's goal of universal health care, and the idea that it's a cost-cutter. Can't happen. Won't happen. Costs are going to *explode*.

An Expensive and Bossy Plan

Think of it: Can anyone name a federal program that ever cut costs for *anything*? Let's not forget that the existing Medicare system is roughly *$80 trillion* in the hole.

And does anybody believe Obama's new "public" health-insurance plan isn't really a bridge to single-payer government-run health care? And does anyone think this plan won't produce a government gatekeeper that will allocate health services *and* control prices *and* therefore crowd-out the private-insurance doctor/hospital system?

Federal boards are going to decide what's good for you and me. And what's *not* good for you and me. These boards will drive a wedge between doctors and patients.

The president, in his *New York Times Magazine* interview with David Leonhardt, said his elderly mother should not (in theory) have had a hip-replacement operation. Yes, Obama would have fought for that operation for his mother's sake. But a federal board of so-called experts would have told the rest of us, "No way."

And then there's the charade of all those private health providers visiting the White House and promising $2 trillion in savings. Utter nonsense.

Universal Health Care Will Bankrupt the Nation

Social Security and Medicare are in financial ruin. Medicare is paying out more than is collected and will be bankrupt in 2017. In 2016 Social Security will start paying out more than it collects; it will be bankrupt in 2037. The Pension Benefit Guaranty Corp., the government agency that insures the pensions of 44 million Americans, has amassed a record $33.5 billion deficit. . . . We are drowning in debt. I ask you: Where are we going to get the money for socialized medicine with this growing deficit?

Colette Worsman, "Socialized Medicine Will Bankrupt Us," *Concord (NH) Monitor*, May 31, 2009. www.concordmonitor.com/article/socialized-medicine-will-bankrupt-us.

The author claims the United States cannot afford the health care plan championed by President Barack Obama.

And even if you put aside the demerits of a government-run health system, Obama's health-care "funding" plans are completely falling apart. Not only will Obama's health program cost at least twice as much as his $650 billion estimate, but his original plan to fund the program by auctioning off carbon-emissions warrants (through the misbegotten cap-and-trade system) has fallen through. In an attempt to buy off hundreds of energy, industrial, and other companies, the White House is now going to give away those

Health Care Is Not America's Most Pressing Issue

A 2010 poll revealed that health care is low on Americans' list of pressing concerns for the country. Americans are much more concerned with adding jobs to the economy and addressing problems in the federal budget and education than they are with the issue of health care.

Question:
"Which of the following is the most important issue facing the country today?"

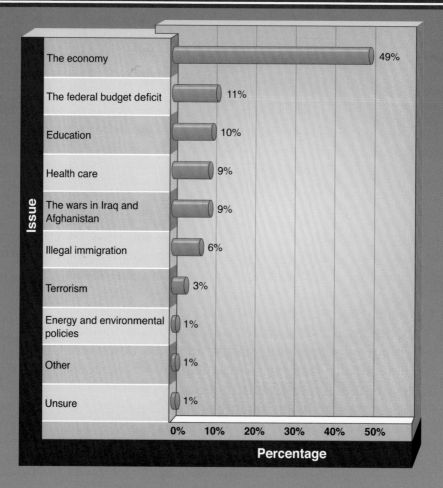

Taken from: CNN/Opinion Research Corporation poll, September 21–23, 2010.

carbon-cap-emissions trading warrants. So all those revenues are out the window. Fictitious.

Anyway, the cap-and-tax system won't pass Congress. The science is wrong. The economics are root-canal austerity—Malthusian[1] limits to growth. And there are too many oil and coal senators who will vote against it.

Universal Health Care Will Bankrupt the Country

All of this is why the national-health-care debate is so outrageous. At some point we have to get serious about solving Medicare by limiting middle-class benefits and funding the program properly. There is no other way out. We can *grow* our way out of the Social Security deficit if we pursue pro-growth policies that maintain low tax and inflation rates. Prospects for that don't look any too good right now, though it could be done. But government health care is nothing but a massive, unfunded, middle-class entitlement problem. (The poor are already in Medicaid.)

Sen. Max Baucus (D., Mont.) proposes to solve health care by limiting employer tax breaks. He's on to something, but he's only got half the story. *All* the tax breaks for health care should go to individuals and small businesses. Let them shop around for the best health deal wherever they can find it with essentially pre-tax dollars.

Additionally, insurance companies should be permitted to sell their products across state lines. And popular health savings accounts—which combine investor retirements with proper insurance by removing the smothering red tape—should be promoted. This approach of consumer choice and market competition will *strengthen* our private health-care system.

---

1. The author is referring to Thomas Robert Malthus, a British economic, political, social, and scientific thinker who believed that population tends to grow faster than the resources on the planet can provide for it, and so must be checked or curbed in some way.

Montana senator Max Baucus plans to solve health care by restricting employer tax breaks.

So private enterprise can coexist with public health care and not be crowded out by the heavy-handed over-reach of government. But the Obama Democrats are determined to force through a state-run system that will bankrupt the country.

Spending Is Already Out of Control

I'm not somebody who obsesses about the national debt or deficit. But I have to admit: Today's spending-and-borrowing is blowing my mind. As a share of GDP [gross domestic product], we're looking at double-digit deficits as far as the eye can see. Over the next ten years, the CBO [Congressional Budget Office] predicts federal debt in the hands of the public will absorb *80 percent* of GDP. And that doesn't include the real cost of state-run health care. Other than the temporary financial conditions surrounding [World War II], we've never seen anything like this.

The president's grandiose government-takeover-and-control strategies are going to make things worse and worse—that is, unless members of that tiny band known as the Republican party [GOP] can stand on their hind legs and just say no. The Republicans must come up with some pro-competition, private-enterprise alternatives for health, energy, education, taxes, and trade that will meet the yearning of voter-taxpayers for a return to private-enterprise American prosperity and opportunity.

Free-market competition will lower costs in health care just as it has every place else. It also will grow the economy. The GOP must return to this basic conservative principle and reject Obama's massive government assault.

Analyze the essay:

1. Kudlow's main opposition to public health care is that it would cost an already struggling nation too much money. Do you think public health care is something Americans should be willing to pay for? Why or why not?

2. Kudlow says a universal health care program would be too expensive, as evidenced by Medicare, the government health care program for seniors, which is currently over budget and underfunded. How would Joel A. Harrison, author of the following viewpoint, respond to this argument? Quote from at least one of the authors in your answer.

Universal Health Care Will Save Americans Money

Joel A. Harrison

Adopting universal health care can save Americans millions of dollars argues Joel A. Harrison in the following essay. He explains that Americans are already paying enormous amounts to the health care system. Yet much of this money is wasted on paperwork, enrollment procedures, commissions, health insurance company salaries, and other bureaucratic aspects of the for-profit system. Harrison says that offering a universal health care plan would streamline many of these money-wasting processes and put more of each dollar toward addressing peoples' health. Harrison believes that Americans can simultaneously lower their health care costs and improve the quality and functioning of the health care system.

Harrison is a San Diego–based consultant who works in the areas of preventive medicine, infectious disease, medical outcomes research, and clinical practice guidelines.

Consider the following questions:

1. According to the author, what percentage of America's 2006 gross domestic product (GDP) was spent on health care costs?
2. How many trillions of tax dollars does Harrison say annual US health care expenses account for?
3. Why does the author think it is unfair to characterize Medicare as a frighteningly expensive program?

Joel A. Harrison, "Paying More, Getting Less," *Dollars and Sense*, May 8, 2008. Reproduced by permission of Dollars and Sense, a progressive economics magazine. www.dollarsandsense.org.

By any measure, the United States spends an enormous amount of money on health care. Here are a few of those measures. In 2006, U.S. health care spending exceeded 16% of the nation's GDP [gross domestic product]. To put U.S. spending into perspective: the United States spent 15.3% of GDP on health care in 2004, while Canada spent 9.9%, France 10.7%, Germany 10.9%, Sweden 9.1%, and the United Kingdom 8.7%. Or consider per capita spending: the United States spent $6,037 per person in 2004, compared to Canada at $3,161, France at $3,191, Germany at $3,169, and the U.K. at $2,560.

The Current System Is Too Expensive to Maintain

By now the high overall cost of health care in the United States is broadly recognized. And many Americans are acutely aware of how much they pay for their own care.

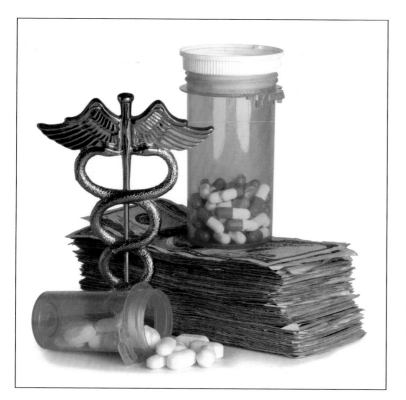

Americans are paying large amounts for health care, and some believe a universal system would save millions of dollars.

America Spends More on Health Care than Any Other Nation

Despite the fact that the United States is the only industrialized nation that does not ensure that all its citizens have health care coverage, the United States spends a much higher percentage of its gross domestic product (GDP) on health care than its peers. It also spends much more per person on health care than its peers.

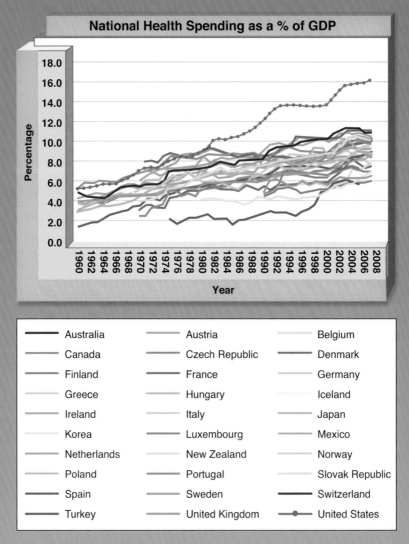

National Health Spending as a % of GDP

Australia	Austria	Belgium
Canada	Czech Republic	Denmark
Finland	France	Germany
Greece	Hungary	Iceland
Ireland	Italy	Japan
Korea	Luxembourg	Mexico
Netherlands	New Zealand	Norway
Poland	Portugal	Slovak Republic
Spain	Sweden	Switzerland
Turkey	United Kingdom	United States

Taken from: Organization for Economic Cooperation and Development, and Catherine Rampell, "U.S. Health Spending Breaks from the Pack," New York Times, July 8, 2009.

Those without health insurance face sky-high doctor and hospital bills and ever more aggressive collection tactics—when they receive care at all. Those who are fortunate enough to have insurance experience steep annual premium hikes along with rising deductibles and co-pays, and, all too often, a well-founded fear of losing their coverage should they lose a job or have a serious illness in the family.

Still, Americans may well *underestimate* the degree to which they subsidize the current U.S. health care system out of their own pockets. And almost no one recognizes that even people without health insurance pay substantial sums into the system today. If more people understood the full size of the health care bill that they as individuals are already paying—and for a system that provides seriously inadequate care to millions of Americans—then the corporate opponents of a universal single-payer system might find it far more difficult to frighten the public about the costs of that system. In other words, to recognize the advantages of a single-payer system, we have to understand how the United States funds health care and health research and how much it actually costs us today.

Health Care Is Already Subsidized Through Taxes

The U.S. health care system is typically characterized as a largely private-sector system, so it may come as a surprise that more than 60% of the $2 trillion annual U.S. health care bill is paid through taxes, according to a 2002 analysis published in *Health Affairs* by Harvard Medical School associate professors Steffie Woolhandler and David Himmelstein. Tax dollars pay for Medicare and Medicaid, for the Veterans Administration and the Indian Health Service. Tax dollars pay for health coverage for

> ## Not Getting What We Have Paid For
>
> We already have socialized medicine and we are already paying for it—twice: once in taxes and once privately. What we are not getting is universal coverage.
>
> Randall Hoven, "A Conservative Case for Universal Health Coverage," *American Thinker*, December 12, 2007. www.americanthinker.com/2007/12/a_conservative_case_for_univer.html.

federal, state, and municipal government employees and their families, as well as for many employees of private companies working on government contracts. Less visible but no less important, the tax deduction for employer-paid health insurance, along with other health care-related tax deductions, also represents a form of government spending on health care. It makes little difference whether the government gives taxpayers (or their employers) a deduction for their health care spending, on the one hand, or collects their taxes then pays for their health care, either directly or via a voucher, on the other. Moreover, tax dollars also pay for critical elements of the health care system apart from direct care—Medicare funds much of the expensive equipment hospitals use, for instance, along with all medical residencies.

Some believe Medicare provides a good model for a universal, single-payer health care system.

All told, then, tax dollars already pay for at least $1.2 trillion in annual U.S. health care expenses. Since federal, state, and local governments collected approximately $3.5 trillion in taxes of all kinds—income, sales, property, corporate—in 2006, that means that *more than one third* of the aggregate tax revenues collected in the United States that year went to pay for health care.

Beyond their direct payments to health care providers and health insurance companies, then, Americans already make a sizeable annual payment into the health care system via taxes. . . .

Much Money Is Wasted on Bureaucracy

After you've finished gasping in surprise at the share of your income that is already going into health care, you may wonder where all that money goes. One answer is that the United States has the most bureaucratic health care system in the world, including over 1,500 different companies, each offering multiple plans, each with its own marketing program and enrollment procedures, its own paperwork and policies, its CEO [chief executive officer] salaries, sales commissions, and other non-clinical costs—and, of course, if it is a for-profit company, its profits. Compared to the overhead costs of the single-payer approach, this fragmented system takes almost 25 cents more out of every health care dollar for expenses other than actually providing care.

Of the additional overhead in the current U.S. system, approximately half is borne by doctors' offices and hospitals, which are forced to maintain large billing and negotiating staffs to deal with all the plans. By contrast, under Canada's single-payer system (which is run by the provinces, not by the federal government), each medical specialty organization negotiates once a year with the nonprofit payer for each province to set fees, and doctors and hospitals need only bill that one payer.

Medicare Is a Good Model

Of course, the United States already has a universal, single-payer health care program: Medicare. Medicare, which serves the elderly and people with disabilities, operates with overhead costs equal to just 3% of total expenditures, compared to 15% to 25% overhead in private health programs. Since Medicare collects its revenue through the IRS [Internal Revenue Service], there is no need to collect from individuals, groups, or businesses. Some complexity remains—after all, Medicare must exist in the fragmented world that is American health care—but no matter how creative the opponents of single-payer get, there is no way they can show convincingly how the administrative costs of a single-payer system could come close to the current level.

Some opponents use current U.S. government expenditures for Medicare and Medicaid to arrive at frightening cost estimates for a universal single-payer health care system. They may use Medicare's $8,568 per person, or $34,272 for a family of four (2006). But they fail to mention that Medicare covers a very atypical, high-cost slice of the U.S. population: senior citizens, regardless of pre-existing conditions, and people with disabilities, including diagnoses such as AIDS and end-stage renal disease. Or they use Medicaid costs—forgetting to mention that half of Medicaid dollars pay for nursing homes, while the other half of Medicaid provides basic health care coverage, primarily to children in low-income households, at a cost of only about $1,500 a year per child.

Universal Health Care Can Save Everyone Money

Americans spend more than anyone else in the world on health care. Each health insurer adds its bureaucracy, profits, high corporate salaries, advertising, and sales commissions to the actual cost of providing care. Not only is this money lost to health care, but it pays for a

Spending More but Getting Less

The United States spends more on health care per person than any other industrialized nation. Despite how much they spend, Americans see the doctor less and have a lower life expectancy than many of their foreign counterparts.

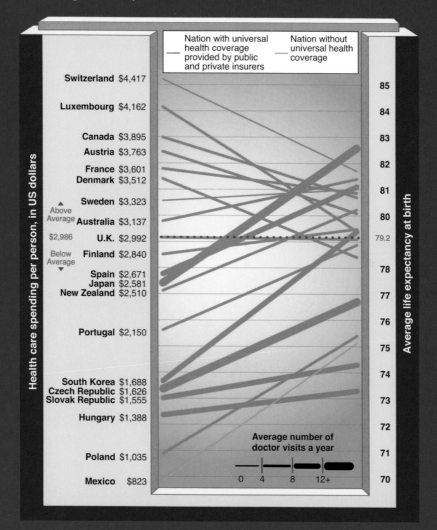

Dollar figures reflect all public and private spending on care, from doctor visits to hospital infrastructure. Data are from 2007 or the most recent year available.

All 30 OECD countries not shown.

Taken from: *National Geographic*, "OECD Health Data 2009." Organization for Economic Co-Operation and Development.

system that often makes it more difficult and complicated to receive the care we've already paid for. Shareholders are the primary clients of for-profit insurance companies, not patients. Moreover, households' actual costs as a percentage of their incomes are far higher today than most imagine. Even families with no health insurance contribute substantially to our health care system through taxes. Recognizing these hidden costs that U.S. households pay for health care today makes it far easier to see how a universal single-payer system—with all of its obvious advantages—can cost most Americans less than the one we have today.

Analyze the essay:

1. Harrison's goal was to convince you to agree with him that a universal health care system can save Americans money. What tools did he use to accomplish this goal? Name at least two persuasive tools used in the essay, and state whether Harrison convinced you to agree with him.

2. The author of the previous essay, Larry Kudlow, warned that a government-run health care program would put Americans at the mercy of a federal board of medical experts. This board could, in theory, make decisions about peoples' health that are not necessarily in their best interest. How do you think Harrison would respond to this concern? Do you think it is a valid concern? Why or why not?

Universal Health Care Will Improve the Quality of Medical Care

Carolyn Lochhead

Carolyn Lochhead is a reporter for the *San Francisco Chronicle*. In the following essay she argues that universal health care can result in higher-quality care for Americans. She examines the situation in Europe, where several governments have adopted universal health care programs. According to Lochhead, these programs are run with significantly smaller budgets than the American health care system has. In addition, they cover more people. Lochhead says that Europeans enjoy greater access to hospitals and doctors who do not make decisions based on profits, but rather what their patients truly need. For all of these reasons Lochhead concludes that adopting a universal health care system modeled after those in Europe could result in higher-quality care for all Americans.

Consider the following questions:

1. What three nations does Lochhead say have high-quality universal health care?
2. What percentage of their national incomes do most European nations spend on health care, according to the author? How many of their citizens does this cover?
3. How much more does the average hospital stay cost in the United States than in Switzerland, according to Lochhead?

Carolyn Lochhead, "Health Care Lessons from Europe," *San Francisco Chronicle*, November 11, 2009. Reproduced by permission.

As Congress struggles to reform U.S. health care, critics point to Canada and Britain as the poster children of what could happen here with a "government takeover" of health coverage.

But three other wealthy nations—the Netherlands, Switzerland and Germany—offer much closer parallels, as well as lessons.

Lessons from Abroad

Health care systems in the three nations more closely resemble the U.S. system of insurance-based coverage. Holland and Switzerland rely exclusively on private insurance, and all three rely on private doctors. The three European nations deliver universal coverage and world-class quality at a fraction of what Americans spend.

All of them require that everyone purchase insurance, make sure everyone can afford it and ban insurers from such practices as refusing to cover the sick that are common in the United States.

"We've got something worse than socialized medicine in this country," said Alain Enthoven, a Stanford University economist known as the father of the Dutch system.

"We have doctors causing hospital infections by not washing their hands because the incentives don't punish them for hospital infections, and we've got something that is financially destroying our economy. It's a disaster."

In many ways, the legislation in Congress builds on a broken system, experts said, reinforcing such features as relying on employers to buy health insurance rather than letting workers shop for their own plans.

European health care is universal, but contrary to popular perception, it is not all nationalized. Facing rapidly aging populations, many European countries have gone much further than the United States in using market forces to control costs. At the same time, regulations are stronger and often more sophisticated.

European, US Health Care Compared

Health care systems in Europe vary widely, but all provide universal coverage for less money than the United States spends, even though populations are older.

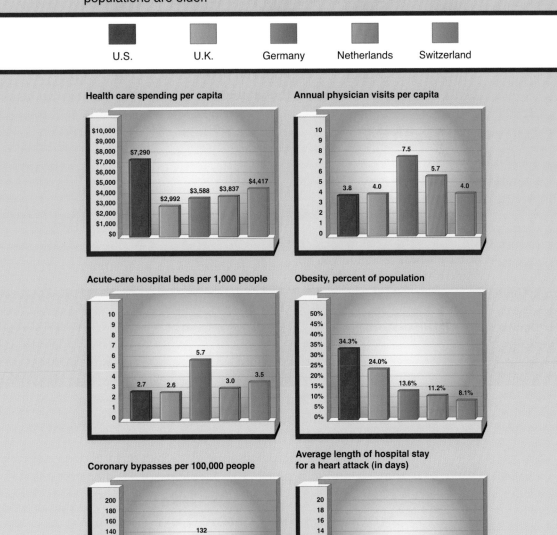

Legend: U.S. | U.K. | Germany | Netherlands | Switzerland

Health care spending per capita

U.S.	U.K.	Germany	Netherlands	Switzerland
$7,290	$2,992	$3,588	$3,837	$4,417

Annual physician visits per capita

U.S.	U.K.	Germany	Netherlands	Switzerland
3.8	4.0	7.5	5.7	4.0

Acute-care hospital beds per 1,000 people

U.S.	U.K.	Germany	Netherlands	Switzerland
2.7	2.6	5.7	3.0	3.5

Obesity, percent of population

U.S.	U.K.	Germany	Netherlands	Switzerland
34.3%	24.0%	13.6%	11.2%	8.1%

Coronary bypasses per 100,000 people

U.S.	U.K.	Germany	Netherlands	Switzerland
85	45	132	58	31

Average length of hospital stay for a heart attack (in days)

U.S.	U.K.	Germany	Netherlands	Switzerland
5.4	8.9	11.0	7.1	7.9

Taken from: Carolyn Lochhead, "Health Care lessons from Europe," *San Francisco Chronicle*, November 29, 2009.

More Doctors, More Beds, More Patient Visits

Most of Europe spends about 10 percent of its national income on health care and covers everyone. The United States will spend 18 percent this year [2009] and leave 47 million people uninsured.

Europe has more doctors, more hospital beds and more patient visits than the United States. Take Switzerland: 4.9 doctors per thousand residents compared with 2.4 in the United States. And cost? The average cost for a hospital stay is $9,398 in relatively high-cost Switzerland and $17,206 in the United States.

"In Switzerland, rich or poor, they all buy the same health insurance," said Regina Herzlinger, chairwoman of business administration at Harvard University and a leading advocate of the Swiss system. "The government gives the poor as much money as the average Swiss has to buy health insurance."

The Swiss and Dutch buy their own coverage from competing private insurers. Both systems address market failures that pervade U.S. health care: Insurance companies must provide a core benefit package and everyone must buy coverage. Consumers can shop for value and pocket the savings, as opposed to U.S. patients who hand the bill to someone else. Switzerland does not have a public program like Medicare or Medicaid.

Americans Suffer from Low-Quality Care

Far from leading to poor quality and rationing, both countries and Germany, where government has a much larger role in health care, outperform the United States on many quality measures. These are not just broad measures such as life expectancy that could reflect higher U.S. poverty or obesity. Even Britain, much maligned by

---

Universal Health Care Will Improve the Quality of Medical Care

Quality care shouldn't depend on your financial resources, or the type of job you have, or the medical condition you face. Every American should be able to get the same treatment that U.S. senators are entitled to.

Ted Kennedy, "'The Cause of My Life,'" *Newsweek*, July 17, 2009. www.newsweek.com/2009/07/17/the-cause-of-my-life.html.

opponents of government-run health care in America, has made greater strides in preventive care.

"The data are pretty clear," said Peter Hussey, a Rand Corp. analyst. "Everybody (in the United States) is at risk for poor-quality care."

Americans often confuse intensive care with quality, said Beth Docteur, a consultant and former health official at the Organization for Economic Cooperation and Development, a group of 30 industrialized countries.

Switzerland has a universal health care system that provides more hospital beds and doctors than the United States does.

U.S. doctors face powerful economic incentives to do more, whether or not it improves a patient's health. These include fee-for-service payments that reward volume, fears of malpractice lawsuits that encourage more tests and procedures, and heavy marketing by drug and device makers.

The Germans apply especially rigorous scientific analysis to determine which medical procedures work and which don't. Critics here argue that such "comparative effectiveness research" leads to rationing or even "death panels." Recommendations this month [November 2009] by a U.S. government panel to cut back on mammograms [breast cancer screenings] have heightened such fears.

Karl Lauterach, director of the Institute of Health Economics at Germany's University of Cologne, described Germany's approach as "protecting patients against ineffective and highly inefficient care."

"If Americans experience a more intensive medicine, is this higher quality? The answer is absolutely not," Docteur said. "A lot of these surgeries and procedures may not even be appropriate for the patient. People are being exposed to risks of hospitalization and risks of adverse events that can exceed the actual benefits."

Covering the Sick Can Be Profitable

The Dutch address what experts consider a critical market failure: The profit-maximizing incentive among health insurers to dump sick people. In Holland, insurers can profit by covering the sick. Some even market plans to diabetics, a practice that would be unthinkable here. The Dutch do this through a complex scheme that pays insurers more for covering the sick.

"Get this wrong, and your public option will fail," warned Cathy Van Beek, acting chairwoman of the executive board of the Dutch Healthcare Authority. Health care reform, she said, "is highly complex and requires great time and effort to get things partly right some of the time."

Legislation in Congress would borrow from the Dutch by creating an "exchange" where some people could buy insurance. But Enthoven believes these are doomed to fail because they are missing key ingredients of the Dutch plan such as access for all.

Moreover, "there is virtually nothing in the bills that is going to control costs," said Gerard Anderson, a professor at the Johns Hopkins Bloomberg School of Public Health. On the plus side, he said, "In terms of making sure people are insured and making sure that you can't be denied coverage, that's much more like the European systems."

Analyze the essay:

1. Lochhead quotes from several sources to support the points she makes in her essay. Make a list of all the people she quotes, including their credentials and the nature of their comments. Then pick the quote you found most persuasive. Why did you choose it? What did it lend to Lochhead's argument?

2. Lochhead's main point is that universal health care can result in higher-quality care for all Americans. For each of the authors in this section, write one or two sentences on what they would think of this assertion. Then, state your own opinion on the matter. Do you think universal health care would result in higher- or lower-quality health care? Why?

Universal Health Care Will Worsen the Quality of Medical Care

Michael Tanner and Michael Cannon

In the following essay Michael Tanner and Michael Cannon argue that universal health care will not improve the quality of medical care in the United States. They explain that simply guaranteeing people access to health insurance does not necessarily mean they will be able to access care when they need it. They point to Europe, where universal health care programs cover 100 percent of the citizenry in some nations. But Tanner and Cannon say that in these countries, people must wait weeks, even months, to receive the care they need. Moreover, these nations experience critical doctor and equipment shortages because they cannot care for everyone adequately. The authors conclude that offering universal health care is not the best way to fix problems in America's health care system.

Michael Tanner is the director of health and welfare studies at the Cato Institute, a libertarian think tank in Washington, D.C., where Michael Cannon is the director of health policy studies.

Consider the following questions:

1. According to Tanner and Cannon, how many weeks must some Swedes wait for heart surgery?
2. Who is Beverly McLachlin and how does she factor into the authors' argument?
3. What did a 2006 study published in the *New England Journal of Medicine* find about the relationship between health insurance and quality of care, as reported by Tanner and Cannon?

Michael Tanner and Michael Cannon, "Universal Healthcare's Dirty Little Secrets," CATO.org, April 5, 2007. Reproduced by permission of The Cato Institute.

As they tack left and right state by state [during the 2008 election campaigns], the Democratic presidential contenders can't agree on much. But one cause they all support—along with Republicans such as former Massachusetts Gov. Mitt Romney and California's own Gov. Arnold Schwarzenegger—is universal health coverage. And all of them are wrong.

What these politicians and many other Americans fail to understand is that there's a big difference between universal coverage and actual access to medical care.

Coverage Does Not Guarantee Care

Simply saying that people have health insurance is meaningless. Many countries provide universal insurance but deny critical procedures to patients who need them. Britain's Department of Health reported in 2006 that at any given time, nearly 900,000 Britons are waiting for admission to National Health Service hospitals,

The wait for heart surgery in Sweden can be up to twenty-five weeks.

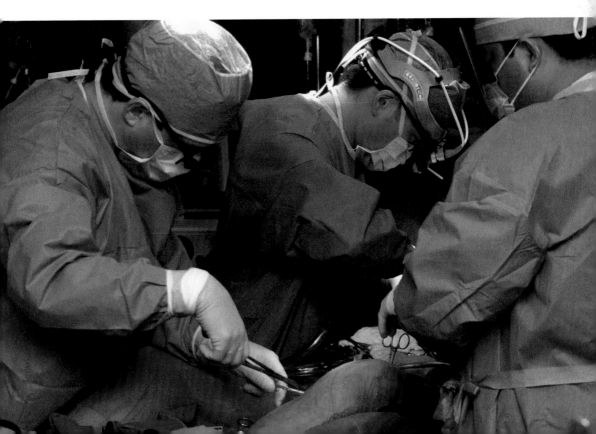

and shortages force the cancellation of more than 50,000 operations each year. In Sweden, the wait for heart surgery can be as long as 25 weeks, and the average wait for hip replacement surgery is more than a year. Many of these individuals suffer chronic pain, and judging by the numbers, some will probably die awaiting treatment. In a 2005 ruling of the Canadian Supreme Court, Chief Justice Beverly McLachlin wrote that "access to a waiting list is not access to healthcare."

Supporters of universal coverage fear that people without health insurance will be denied the healthcare they need. Of course, all Americans already have access to at least emergency care. Hospitals are legally obligated to provide care regardless of ability to pay, and although physicians do not face the same legal requirements, we do not hear of many who are willing to deny treatment because a patient lacks insurance.

> ## The Government Should Not Be in Charge of Our Health
>
> Once the government gets into the business of providing our health care, the government gets into the business of deciding whose life matters, and how much. It gets into the business of deciding what we 'really' want, when what we really want can never be a second chocolate éclair that might make us a size fourteen and raise the cost of treating us.
>
> Megan McCardle, "Why I Oppose National Health Care," *Atlantic*, July 28, 2009. www.theatlantic.com/business/archive/2009/07/why-i-oppose-national-health-care/22300/.

Being Insured Does Not Result in Better Health

You may think it is self-evident that the uninsured may forgo preventive care or receive a lower quality of care. And yet, in reviewing all the academic literature on the subject, Helen Levy of the University of Michigan's Economic Research Initiative on the Uninsured, and David Meltzer of the University of Chicago, were unable to establish a "causal relationship" between health insurance and better health. Believe it or not, there is "no evidence," Levy and Meltzer wrote, that expanding insurance coverage is a cost-effective way to promote health. Similarly, a study published in the *New England Journal of Medicine* last year [2006] found that, although far too many Americans were not receiving the appropriate stan-

dard of care, "health insurance status was largely unre-
lated to the quality of care."

Another common concern is that the young and
healthy will go without insurance, leaving a risk pool of
older and sicker people. This results in higher insurance
premiums for those who are insured. But that's only true
if the law forbids insurers from charging their customers
according to the cost of covering them. If companies can
charge more to cover people who are likely to need more
care—smokers, the elderly, etc.—then it won't make any
difference who does or doesn't buy insurance.

Finally, some suggest that when people without
health insurance receive treatment, the cost of their
care is passed along to the rest of us. This is undeni-
ably true. Yet, it is a manageable problem. According

*A volunteer provides
those in a hospital
waiting room with a
cup of coffee to enjoy
during their wait.*

to Jack Hadley and John Holahan of the left-leaning Urban Institute, uncompensated care for the uninsured amounts to less than 3% of total healthcare spending—a real cost, no doubt, but hardly a crisis.

Covering All Americans Is the Wrong Solution

Everyone agrees that far too many Americans lack health insurance. But covering the uninsured comes about as a by-product of getting other things right. The real danger is that our national obsession with universal coverage will lead us to neglect reforms—such as enacting a standard health insurance deduction, expanding health savings accounts and deregulating insurance markets—that could truly expand coverage, improve quality and make care more affordable.

As [essayist] H. L. Mencken said: "For every problem, there is a solution that is simple, elegant, and wrong." Universal healthcare is a textbook case.

Analyze the essay:

1. Tanner and Cannon argue that a key fallacy in the health care debate is that simply guaranteeing people access to insurance means they will be cared for. Do you agree with this assertion? Why or why not?

2. In the previous essay, Carolyn Lochhead said Europe offers an example of how universal health care can result in higher-quality care. But in this essay, Tanner and Cannon describe Europe as a place where people do not receive care in a timely manner. After reading both essays, with which authors do you agree? Why? List at least two pieces of evidence that swayed you.

Section Two: Model Essays and Writing Exercises

The Five-Paragraph Essay

An *essay* is a short piece of writing that discusses or analyzes one topic. The five-paragraph essay is a form commonly used in school assignments and tests. Every five-paragraph essay begins with an *introduction*, ends with a *conclusion*, and features three *supporting paragraphs* in the middle.

The Thesis Statement. The introduction includes the essay's thesis statement. The thesis statement presents the argument or point the author is trying to make about the topic. The essays in this book all have different thesis statements because they are making different arguments about health care.

The thesis statement should clearly tell the reader what the essay will be about. A focused thesis statement helps determine what will be in the essay; the subsequent paragraphs are spent developing and supporting its argument.

The Introduction. In addition to presenting the thesis statement, a well-written introductory paragraph captures the attention of the reader and explains why the topic being explored is important. It may provide the reader with background information on the subject matter or feature an anecdote that illustrates a point relevant to the topic. It could also present startling information that clarifies the point of the essay or puts forth a contradictory position that the essay will refute. Further techniques for writing an introduction are found later in this section.

The Supporting Paragraphs. The introduction is then followed by three (or, in a longer essay, more) supporting paragraphs. These are the main body of the essay. Each paragraph presents and develops a *subtopic* that supports the essay's thesis statement. Each subtopic is spearheaded by a *topic sentence* and supported by its own facts, details, and examples. The writer can use various kinds of supporting material and details to back up the topic of each supporting paragraph. These may include statistics, quotations from people with special knowledge or expertise, historic facts, and anecdotes. A rule of writing is that specific and concrete examples are more convincing than vague, general, or unsupported assertions.

The Conclusion. The conclusion is the paragraph that closes the essay. Its function is to summarize or reiterate the main idea of the essay. It may recall an idea from the introduction or briefly examine the larger implications of the thesis. Because the conclusion is also the last chance a writer has to make an impression on the reader, it is important that it not simply repeat what has been presented elsewhere in the essay but close it in a clear, final, and memorable way.

Although the order of the essay's component paragraphs is important, they do not have to be written in the order presented here. Some writers like to decide on a thesis and write the introduction paragraph first. Other writers like to focus first on the body of the essay, and write the introduction and conclusion later.

Pitfalls to Avoid

When writing essays about controversial issues such as health care, it is important to remember that disputes over the material are common precisely because there are many different perspectives. Remember to state your arguments in careful and measured terms. Evaluate your topic fairly—avoid overstating the negative qualities of one perspective or understating the positive qualities of another. Use examples, facts, and details to support any assertions you make.

The Persuasive Essay

There are many types of essays, but in general, they are usually short compositions in which the writer expresses and discusses an opinion about something. In the persuasive essay the writer tries to persuade the reader to do something or to convince the reader to agree with the writer's opinion about something. Examples of persuasive writing are easy to find. Advertising is one common example. Through commercials and print ads, companies try to persuade the public to buy their products for specific reasons. A lot of everyday writing is persuasive, too. Letters to the editor, posts from sports fans on team websites, even handwritten notes urging a friend to listen to a new CD—all are examples of persuasive writing.

The Tools of Persuasion

The writer of the persuasive essay uses various tools to persuade the reader. Here are some of them:

Facts and statistics. A fact is a statement that no one, typically, would disagree with. It can be verified by information in reputable resources, such as encyclopedias, almanacs, government websites, or reference books.

Examples of Facts and Statistics

Christmas is celebrated on December 25.
Berlin is the capital of Germany.
Twenty percent of all pregnancies end in miscarriage.
According to an ABC News/*Washington Post* poll, 74 percent of Americans believe that the United States is not doing enough to prevent illegal aliens from entering the country.

It is important to note that facts and statistics can be *misstated* (written down or quoted incorrectly), *misinterpreted* (not understood correctly by the user), or *misused* (not used fairly). But, if a writer uses facts and statistics properly, they can add authority to the writer's essay.

Opinions. An opinion is what a person thinks about something. It can be contested or argued with; however, opinions of people who are experts on the topic or who have personal experience are often very convincing. Many persuasive essays are written to convince the reader that the writer's opinion is worth believing and acting on.

Testimonials. A testimonial is a statement given by a person who is thought to be an expert or who has another trait people admire, such as being a celebrity. Television commercials frequently use testimonials to persuade watchers to buy the products they are advertising.

Examples. An example is something that is representative of a group or type (a Labrador retriever is an example of the group "dog"). Examples are used to help define, describe, or illustrate something to make it more understandable.

Anecdotes. Anecdotes are extended examples. They are little stories with a beginning, middle, and end. They can be used just like examples to explain something or to exemplify something about a topic.

Appeals to reason. One way to convince readers that an opinion or action is right is to appeal to reason or logic. This often involves a process of reasoning that states that if one idea is true, then another must also be true. Here is an example of one type of appeal to reason:

— Eating fast food causes obesity and diabetes, just as smoking cigarettes causes lung cancer and asthma. For this reason, fast food companies, like cigarette manufacturers, should be held legally responsible for their customers' health.

Appeals to emotion. Another way to convince or persuade readers to believe or to do something is to appeal to their emotions—love, fear, pity, loyalty, and anger are some of the emotions to which writers appeal. A writer who wants to persuade someone not to eat meat might appeal to their love of animals:

— If you own a cat, dog, hamster, or bird, you should not eat meat. It makes no sense to pamper and love your pet while at the same time supporting the merciless slaughter of other animals for your dinner.

Ridicule and name-calling. Although some writers may use them, ridicule and name-calling are not good techniques to use in a persuasive essay. Instead of exploring the strengths of the topic, the writer who uses these relies on making those who oppose the main idea look foolish, evil, or stupid. In most cases, the writer who does this weakens his or her argument.

Bandwagon. The writer who uses the bandwagon technique uses the idea that "everybody thinks this or is doing this; therefore it is valid." The bandwagon method is not a very authoritative way to convince your reader of your point.

Words and Phrases Common to Persuasive Essays

accordingly	it stands to reason
because	it then follows that
clearly	obviously
consequently	since
for this reason	subsequently
indeed	therefore
it is necessary to	this is why
it makes sense to	thus
it seems clear that	we must

Dr. Government? Why Universal Health Care Is Bad for America

Editor's Notes Persuasive essays typically try to get a reader to agree with the author's point of view. This is the goal of the following model essay. It argues that universal health care is bad for America, and offers three supporting reasons. The essay is structured as a five-paragraph essay in which each paragraph contributes a piece of evidence to develop the argument.

The notes in the margin point out key features of the essay and will help you understand how the essay is organized. Also note that all sources are cited using Modern Language Association (MLA) style.* For more information on how to cite your sources see Appendix C. In addition, consider the following:

Refers to thesis and topic sentences

Refers to supporting details

1. How does the introduction engage the reader's attention?
2. What persuasive techniques are used in the essay?
3. What purpose do the essay's quotes serve?
4. Does the essay convince you of its point?

Paragraph 1

Universal health care sounds great in theory: All those without another form of insurance can be covered by a government program, and no one will be without care when they need it. But when you really think about it, such a prospect is a disaster waiting to happen. Establishing universal health care will be prohibitively expensive, overcrowd the health system, and even threaten our freedom.

This is the essay's thesis statement. It tells the reader what will be argued in the following paragraphs.

* Editor's Note: In applying MLA style guidelines in this book, the following simplifications have been made: Parenthetical text citations are confined to direct quotations only; electronic source documentation in the Works Cited list omits date of access, page ranges, and some detailed facts of publication.

Paragraph 2

Offering universal health care is a prohibitively expensive endeavor. "Does anybody really believe that adding 50 million people to the public health-care rolls will *not* cost the government more money?" asks economist Larry Kudlow. "About $1.5 trillion to $2 trillion more? At least." (Kudlow) Kudlow is right: Anyone who thinks that universal health care will not tax an already broke nation is fooling themselves. The best evidence for this is Medicare, the government-funded health insurance program that covers senior citizens and the disabled. As of September 2010, Medicare covered 47 million Americans—and was underfunded by trillions of dollars. Clearly the government is unable to pay for the people it is already charged with covering and cannot afford to cover any more.

Paragraph 3

In addition, offering everyone health insurance is likely to overcrowd the health system, making it harder for people to receive timely care. Michael Tanner and Michael Cannon, of the Cato Institute, point out that the quality of health care suffers in nations that offer their citizens universal health insurance. In Britain, for example, they report that tens of thousands of surgeries are cancelled each year because there are not enough doctors to perform them and not enough hospital space to accommodate them. In Sweden, another nation with universal health insurance, people wait as long as six months, even a year, to receive critical surgeries and transplants. "Many of these individuals suffer chronic pain, and judging by the numbers, some will probably die awaiting treatment." (Tanner and Cannon)

Paragraph 4

Finally, inviting the government into the business of health threatens all Americans' freedoms. Health and health care are very private matters. People indulge in unhealthy vices all the time—they smoke, they eat fast food, they choose not to exercise. As Americans, they are free to do this. Caring for these people when they get sick is expensive, but we support their right to take such risks. No one wants to be forced to exercise on a daily basis or be told what to eat. But once the government is covering its citizens' health care, it adopts a vested interest in making sure they take better, less-expensive care of themselves, and this involves restricting their freedom to live their lives as unhealthily as they choose. "Once the government gets into the business of providing our health care," writes one economics adviser, "it gets into the business of deciding what we 'really' want, where what we really want can never be a second chocolate éclair that might make us a size fourteen and raise the cost of treating us." (McCardle) Putting the government in the position of being both lawmaker and health provider means it will inevitably use its power to save money at the expense of our freedoms.

Analyze this quote. What do you think made the author want to select it for inclusion in the essay? Offer at least two reasons.

Paragraph 5

The cost, logistics, and restraints of universal health care are but a few reasons to reject it. The prospect of Dr. Government is lose-lose for current and future generations of Americans.

Works Cited

Kudlow, Larry. "Obama's 'Public' Health Plan Will Bankrupt the Nation." *National Review* 13 May 2009.

McCardle, Megan. "Why I Oppose National Health Care." *Atlantic* 28 Jul 2009.

Tanner, Michael, and Michael Cannon. "Universal Healthcare's Dirty Little Secrets." *Los Angeles Times* 5 Apr 2007.

Exercise 1A: Create an Outline from an Existing Essay

It often helps to create an outline of the five-paragraph essay before you write it. The outline can help you organize the information, arguments, and evidence you have gathered during your research.

For this exercise, create an outline that could have been used to write "Dr. Government? Why Universal Health Care Is Bad for America." This "reverse engineering" exercise is meant to help familiarize you with how outlines can help classify and arrange information.

To do this you will need to
1. articulate the essay's thesis,
2. pinpoint important pieces of evidence,
3. flag quotes that supported the essay's ideas, and
4. identify key points that support the argument.

Part of the outline has already been started to give you an idea of the assignment.

Outline

I. Paragraph 1
Write the essay's thesis:

II. Paragraph 2
Topic: Offering universal health care is a prohibitively expensive endeavor.

Supporting Detail i. Quote from Larry Kudlow.

Supporting Detail ii.

III. Paragraph 3
Topic: Offering everyone health insurance is likely to overcrowd the health system, making it harder for people to receive timely care.

Supporting Detail i. In Sweden people wait as long as six months, even a year, to receive critical surgeries and transplants.

Supporting Detail ii.

IV. Paragraph 4
Topic:

Supporting Detail i.

Supporting Detail ii. Quote from Megan McCardle.

V. Paragraph 5
Write the essay's conclusion:

Exercise 1B: Create an Outline for Your Own Essay

The model essay you just read expresses a particular point of view about universal health care. For this exercise, your assignment is to find supporting ideas, choose specific and concrete details, create an outline, and ultimately write a five-paragraph essay making a different, or even opposing, point about universal health care. Your goal is to use persuasive techniques to convince your reader.

Part l: Write a thesis statement.

The following thesis statement would be appropriate for an opposing essay on why universal health care should he adopted:

Universal health care will simultaneously save Americans money while improving their access to and level of care.

Or, see the sample paper topics suggested in Appendix D for more ideas.

Part II: Brainstorm pieces of supporting evidence.

Using information from some of the viewpoints in the previous section and from the information found in Section III of this book, write down three arguments or pieces of evidence that support the thesis statement you selected. Then, for each of these three arguments, write down supportive facts, examples, and details that support it. These could be:

- statistical information
- personal memories and anecdotes
- quotes from experts, peers, or family members
- observations of people's actions and behaviors
- specific and concrete details

Supporting pieces of evidence for the above sample thesis statement are found in this book, and include:

- Points made in Viewpoint Four by Joel A. Harrison about how much money is currently wasted in the health care system by paperwork, enrollment procedures, commissions, health insurance company salaries, and other bureaucratic aspects of the for-profit system.

- Charts accompanying Viewpoint Four that show that America spends more on health care than any other nation, yet is the only industrialized nation that does not offer its citizens universal health care coverage.

- Quote box accompanying Viewpoint Four by Randall Hoven titled, "Not Getting What We Have Paid For." The link to Hoven's full article is www.american thinker.com/2007/12/a_conservative_case_for_univer.html. More information that can support this topic is found there.

Part III: Place the information from Part I in outline form.

Part IV: Write the arguments or supporting statements in paragraph form.

By now you have three arguments that support the paragraph's thesis statement, as well as supporting material. Use the outline to write out your three supporting arguments in paragraph form. Make sure that each paragraph has a topic sentence that states the paragraph's thesis clearly and broadly. Then, add supporting sentences that express the facts, quotes, details, and examples that support the paragraph's argument. The paragraph may also have a concluding or summary sentence.

Spending More to Get Less

Editor's Notes The following model essay argues
that switching to a universal health
care system will save Americans money. Like the first
model essay, this essay is structured as a five-paragraph
persuasive essay in which each paragraph contributes a
supporting piece of evidence to develop the argument.
Each supporting paragraph explores one of three distinct
reasons why the author thinks that the current health care
system costs too much and delivers too little.

As you read this essay, take note of its components
and how they are organized (the sidebars in the margins
provide further explanation).

Paragraph 1

People who say the United States can't afford universal health care don't understand the first thing about
the current cost and status of health care in the United
States. We are the only industrialized nation that does
not ensure that all its citizens have health coverage, and
we receive poorer care than citizens of nations that spend
less. The current system is broken and bankrupting us,
and it is beyond time for change.

This is the topic sen-
tence of Paragraph 2.
Note that all of the
paragraph's details fit
with it, or *support* it.

Paragraph 2

Americans spend more on health care than any other
country in the world. According to the Organisation for
Economic Co-operation and Development, the United
States spends $7,290 on health care per person, in both
taxes and private spending. To say this is more than other
countries is a gross understatement: It is more than twice
what France, Denmark, Sweden, Australia, and the UK
pay; it is more than what South Korea, the Czech Republic,
Hungary, Poland, and Mexico pay *combined*. "Americans
spend more than anyone else in the world on health care,"
writes medical consultant Joel A. Harrison. In his opinion,

What point in Paragraph
2 does this quote direct-
ly support?

a universal health care system "can cost most Americans less than the one we have today." (Harrison)

Paragraph 3

Despite spending more, Americans get much less. Americans see the doctor less often than citizens of other nations, and have poorer life expectancies. Citizens of Japan, for example (where $2,581 is spent on health care per person), visit the doctor more than twelve times per year, and live on average, four to five years longer. The same is true for citizens of South Korea (which spends $1,688 per person), who see the doctor about eight times a year and live, on average, at least a year longer than Americans. Meanwhile, European nations have more doctors and more hospital beds than American facilities, and charge less for hospital visits. In contrast, the Centers for Disease Control and Prevention reports that 6.9 percent of Americans do not even go to the doctor because it costs too much. This doesn't make sense at all—the nation that pays the most should live the longest, get the best care, and see the doctor most often.

This information was taken from the chart that accompanies Viewpoint Four in Section One. This book is filled with information to support points in your essays.

"Meanwhile" is a transitional phrase that keeps the ideas in the essay flowing. Make a list of all transitional words and phrases used in the essay.

Paragraph 4

The Patient Protection and Affordable Care Act, passed by the Obama Administration in 2010, was an excellent move toward reducing the amount America wastes on its broken health care system. It requires that all Americans get health insurance, which will reduce the high cost of caring for the uninsured. It prohibits insurance companies from banning people from getting coverage, which will save people money in outrageous premiums and high deductibles. A December 2010 study by the Commonwealth Fund found that provisions in the new law will save American families more than $3,000 per year by 2020; the law is expected to save the United States $1 trillion over that period.

What is the topic sentence of Paragraph 4? How did you recognize it?

What point in Paragraph 4 does this fact directly support?

Paragraph 5

At these prices, Americans should have a lot more to show for their money. But all we have are empty wal-

What pieces of this essay are opinions? What parts are facts? Make a list of opinions and facts and see which the author relies on more.

lets and sick citizens. "We now have the worst of both worlds," writes one columnist. "We are paying for universal health coverage, but not getting it." (Hoven) It doesn't take a genius to see that America is spending a ton of money and getting very little in return. People who say the United States can't afford universal health care have it backwards: what we can't afford is the status quo.

Works Cited

Harrison, Joel A. "Paying More, Getting Less." *Dollars and Sense* 8 May 2008. < http://dollarsandsense.org/archives/2008/0508harrison.html > Accessed December 26, 2010.

Hoven, Randall. "A Conservative Case for Universal Health Coverage." *American Thinker* 12 Dec. 2007. < http://www.americanthinker.com/2007/12/a_conservative_case_for_univer.html > Accessed December 26, 2010.

Exercise 2A: Create an Outline from an Existing Essay

As you did for the first model essay in this section, create an outline that could have been used to write "Spending More to Get Less." Be sure to identify the essay's thesis statement, its supporting ideas and details, and key pieces of evidence that were used.

Exercise 2B: Identify Persuasive Techniques

Essayists use many techniques to get you to agree with their ideas or to do something they want you to do. Some of the most common techniques are described in Preface B of this section, "The Persuasive Essay." These tools are *facts* and *statistics, opinions, testimonials, examples* and *anecdotes, appeals to reason, appeals to emotion, ridicule* and *name-calling,* and *bandwagon.* Go back to the preface and review these tools. Remember that most of these tools can be used to enhance your essay, but some of them—particularly ridiculing, name-calling, and bandwagon—can detract from the essay's effectiveness. Nevertheless, you should be able to recognize them in the essays you read.

Some writers use one persuasive tool throughout the whole essay. For example, the essay may be one extended anecdote, or the writer may rely entirely on statistics. But most writers typically use a combination of persuasive tools. Model Essay Two, "Spending More to Get Less," does this.

Problem One
Read Model Essay Two again and see whether you can find every persuasive tool used. Put that information in the following table. Part of the table is filled in for you. Explanatory notes are beneath the table. (NOTE: You will not fill in every box. No paragraph contains all of the techniques.)

	Paragraph 1 Sentence #	Paragraph 2 Sentence #	Paragraph 3 Sentence #	Paragraph 4 Sentence #	Paragraph 5 Sentence #
Fact		1a			
Statistic			6b		
Opinion				1d	
Testimonial					
Example					
Anecdote					
Appeal to Reason			7c		
Appeal to Emotion					
Ridicule					5e
Name-Calling					
Bandwagon					

Notes

a. That the United States spends more on health care than any other nation is a *fact*.

b. The finding of the Centers for Disease Control and Prevention that 6.9 percent of Americans do not go to the doctor because it costs too much is a *statistic*.

c. The author is appealing to your sense of reason when she says the nation that pays the most should live the longest, get the best care, and see the doctor most often.

d. That the Patient Protection and Affordable Care Act was "an excellent move" is a matter of opinion; others disagree.

e. The author is ridiculing her opponents when she says "It doesn't take a genius . . ."

Now, look at the table you have produced. Which persuasive tools does this essay rely on most heavily? Which are not used at all?

Problem Two
Apply this exercise to the other model essays in this section, and the viewpoints in Section One, when you are finished reading them.

The Government Can and Should Require Americans to Buy Health Insurance

Editor's Notes The final model essay argues that it is both legal and appropriate for the government to require all Americans to have health insurance. Supported by facts, quotes, statistics, and opinions, it tries to persuade the reader that the individual mandate clause in the 2010 Patient Protection and Affordable Care Act, which requires all Americans to obtain health insurance by 2010 or pay a fine, will reduce health care costs for all Americans.

This essay differs from the previous model essays in that it is longer than five paragraphs. Sometimes five paragraphs are simply not enough to adequately develop an idea. Extending the length of an essay can allow the reader to explore a topic in more depth or present multiple pieces of evidence that together provide a complete picture of a topic. Longer essays can also help readers discover the complexity of a subject by examining a topic beyond its superficial exterior. Moreover, the ability to write a sustained research or position paper is a valuable skill you will need as you advance academically.

As you read, consider the questions posed in the margins. Continue to identify thesis statements, supporting details, transitions, and quotations. Examine the introductory and concluding paragraphs to understand how they give shape to the essay. Finally, evaluate the essay's general structure and assess its overall effectiveness.

■ Refers to thesis and topic sentences

■ Refers to supporting details

Paragraph 1

One of the most controversial pieces of the 2010 Patient Protection and Affordable Care Act (PPACA) was a provision that requires nearly all Americans to have health insurance as of 2014. This piece of the act was imme-

What is the essay's thesis statement? How did you recognize it?

diately picked up as controversial. But there's good reason for such a provision: It will lower health care costs for everyone and is perfectly constitutional, meaning it fits within the philosophical and legal framework of the United States Constitution.

Paragraph 2

Requiring all Americans to have health insurance is significantly less expensive than letting them go without. The uninsured cost money—a lot of money. They cost the health care system money, they cost those who have insurance money, and they cost taxpayers money. According to a report by the Center for American Progress, on average, American families pay approximately $1,100 per year—or about 8 percent of their total 2009 health care premiums—to offset the costs incurred by the uninsured. This is because when uninsured people can't afford to pay, health care providers shift the costs of their care to people who can: those with insurance. These payments come in the form of higher insurance premiums, out-of-pocket costs, and taxes.

What point in Paragraph 2 does this fact directly support?

Paragraph 3

From this perspective, covering the uninsured saves everyone money. While there are some costs associated with requiring uninsured Americans to buy health insurance—for example, the cost of purchasing coverage and paying a fine if they fail to do so—it is significantly more expensive to continue letting millions of Americans go without coverage. Requiring people to have health insurance is not a violation of their rights, but a sound financial strategy for easing the financial burden on those with coverage. "What's at stake isn't Americans' cherished 'right to be let alone,'" write the editors at the *Los Angeles Times*. "It's whether they'll continue to be stuck in a system in which millions of uninsured people force those with insurance to pick up at least part of the tab for their visits to the emergency room and for the untreated diseases that they spread." (*Los Angeles Times*) Lest any-

Analyze this quote. What do you think made the author want to include it in the essay?

one argue that the uninsured are being unfairly forced to pay for coverage they cannot afford, the government has promised to financially assist all those who have to get coverage under the PPACA.

Paragraph 4

In addition to being fiscally responsible, the "individual mandate," or requirement to acquire health insurance, is perfectly constitutional, despite claims to the contrary. In December 2010, Virginia judge Henry E. Hudson caused a stir when he ruled the individual mandate portion of the PPACA unconstitutional. Hudson said that it violates the Interstate Commerce Clause and claimed Congress can't force people to buy something they don't want. And that's true—it is illegal for the government to force someone to buy a dog if they do not want to be dog owner; likewise, it is unthinkable for the government to require someone to buy a certain type of food or any other piece of property that they are not interested in owning or consuming.

> What is the topic sentence of Paragraph 4? How did you recognize it?

Paragraph 5

But the fact is, nearly all Americans—whether they have insurance or not—already participate in the health care industry. Every time someone visits a doctor, goes to the emergency room (with or without insurance), or even buys cold medicine or painkillers at the drug store, they are participating in the health care market. Congress is therefore not forcing anyone to enter a market or industry that they would otherwise not participate in. "[The] individual mandate affects how people pay for the care they consume, but it doesn't force them into the healthcare market—they're already there," explains the editorial board of the *Los Angeles Times*. "If the courts consider the mandate in its proper context, they'll see that it doesn't violate the Constitution." (*Los Angeles Times*)

> What point in Paragraph 5 does this quote support?

Paragraph 6

Other federal judges, such as US district judge George Steeh of Detroit, Michigan, have agreed that it is legal for the government to require individuals to have health insurance. As Steeh explained in his October 2010 ruling, by choosing not to have insurance, people are merely postponing the inevitable purchase of health care services. This is tantamount to "collectively shifting billions of dollars, $43 billion in 2008, onto other market participants." Concluded Steeh, "The uninsured, like plaintiffs, benefit from the 'guaranteed issue' provision in the Act, which enables them to become insured even when they are already sick." (Qtd. in Hersch) In other words, because the PPACA also prohibits insurance companies from refusing to cover people because they have a prior illness or from setting eligibility rules based on gender or current health, all Americans will be insurable. "This benefit makes imposing the minimum coverage provision appropriate," said Steeh. (Qtd. in Hersch)

Paragraph 7

What is the topic sentence of Paragraph 7?

Finally, the PPACA does not unfairly penalize the few Americans who truly do not participate in the health care industry. Indeed, groups such as the Amish or the Mennonites, or others whose religion prevents them from seeking any form of medical care, taking medicine, or paying into Social Security, are exempt from the individual mandate. A slew of legal scholars—including Erwin Chemerinsky (University of California–Irvine School of Law), Mark Hall (Wake Forest University), Jonathan H. Adler (Case Western Reserve University School of Law), Doug Kendall (Constitutional Accountability Center), and Michael Dorf (Cornell University Law School)—argue that this is one of the many terms of the mandate that make it both constitutional and appropriate.

Paragraph 8

Interestingly, while the individual mandate is unpopular, the most popular provisions of the PPACA are only possible if the individual mandate is included. The only way to afford to include risky or expensive-to-treat people in the health care system is to greatly expand the number of nonrisky, nonexpensive-to-treat people in the system as well—and this involves requiring all Americans, even the young and poor, to have insurance. Yet this catch-22 has been lost on the American public. A November 2010 Kaiser Family Foundation poll, for example, found that 68 percent of Americans want the individual mandate part of the law repealed. Yet the same poll found that 71 percent would keep the part of the law that provides financial help to low and moderate income Americans who don't get insurance through their jobs to help them purchase coverage; 71 percent would also keep the part of the law that prohibits insurance companies from denying coverage because of a person's medical history or health condition. Both of these provisions are only financially possible if almost all healthy Americans have insurance.

> Make a list of all the transitions that appear in the essay and how they keep the ideas flowing.

> What pieces of this essay are opinions? What parts are facts? Make a list of opinions and facts and see which the author relies on more.

Paragraph 9

Lastly, for all the fuss that's been raised about this provision, it will affect a relatively small number of people. Indeed, most Americans already have health insurance. The Centers for Disease Control and Prevention reports that nearly 85 percent of Americans are already covered. Sixty-three percent have private insurance, possibly through an employer, while the rest receive coverage through public programs like Medicare or Medicaid. The almost 16 percent of Americans who do not have insurance are the only ones who would be affected by a requirement to get insurance.

> What is the topic sentence of Paragraph 9?

> Identify a piece of evidence used to support Paragraph 9's main idea.

Paragraph 10

In protesting the individual mandate, Republican senator John Ensign asked, "What's next? Will we consider legislation in the future requiring every American to buy a car? Will we consider legislation in the future requiring every American to buy a house?" (Qtd. in Hitt and Bendavid) But requiring Americans to have health insurance is less like requiring them to buy cars and houses and more like requiring them to buy car insurance and home insurance—which we do require. This is the best

After reading the essay, are you convinced of the author's point? If so, what evidence swayed you? If not, why not?

way to ensure that the costs are spread over the largest number of people possible. Critics of the individual mandate provision overlook this critical fact and have made a mountain out of this molehill of an issue.

Works Cited

"The Individual Mandate: It's Constitutional." *Los Angeles Times* 15 Dec. 2010. < http://articles.latimes.com/2010/dec/15/opinion/la-ed-health-20101215 > Accessed December 23, 2010.

Hersch, Warren S. "Judge Upholds PPACA's Individual Mandate—Regulatory, Legislative and Tax Issues." *National Underwriter* 8 Oct. 2010. < http://www.lifeand healthinsurancenews.com/News/2010/10/Pages/Judge-Rules-Upholds-PPACAs-Individual-Mandate.aspx > . Accessed December 23, 2010.

Hitt, Gregg, and Naftali Bendavid. "One Hurdle Remains in Senate." *Wall Street Journal* 23 Dec. 2009: A4.

Exercise 3A: Examining Introductions and Conclusions

Every essay features introductory and concluding paragraphs that are used to frame the main ideas being presented. Along with presenting the essay's thesis statement, well-written introductions should grab the attention of the reader and make clear why the topic being explored is important. The conclusion reiterates the essay's thesis and is also the last chance for the writer to make an impression on the reader. Strong introductions and conclusions can greatly enhance an essay's effect on an audience.

The Introduction

There are several techniques that can be used to craft an introductory paragraph. An essay can start with:

- an anecdote: a brief story that illustrates a point relevant to the topic;
- startling information: facts or statistics that elucidate the point of the essay;
- setting up and knocking down a position: a position or claim believed by proponents of one side of a controversy, followed by statements that challenge that claim;
- historical perspective: an example of the way things used to be that leads into a discussion of how or why things work differently now;
- summary information: general introductory information about the topic that feeds into the essay's thesis statement.

Problem One
Reread the introductory paragraphs of the model essays and of the viewpoints in Section One. Identify which of the techniques described above are used in these essays and viewpoints. How do they grab the attention of the reader? Are their thesis statements clearly presented?

Problem Two

Write an introduction for the essay you have outlined and partially written in Exercise 1B using one of the techniques described above.

The Conclusion

The conclusion brings the essay to a close by summarizing or returning to its main ideas. Good conclusions, however, go beyond simply repeating these ideas. Strong conclusions explore a topic's broader implications and reiterate why it is important to consider. They may frame the essay by returning to an anecdote featured in the opening paragraph. Or, they may close with a quotation or refer back to an event in the essay. In opinionated essays, the conclusion can reiterate which side the essay is taking or ask the reader to reconsider a previously held position on the subject.

Problem Three

Reread the concluding paragraphs of the model essays and of the viewpoints in Section One. Which were most effective in driving their arguments home to the reader? What sorts of techniques did they use to do this? Did they appeal emotionally to the reader, or bookend an idea or event referenced elsewhere in the essay?

Problem Four

Write a conclusion for the essay you have outlined and partially written in Exercise 1B using one of the techniques described above.

Exercise 3B: Using Quotations to Enliven Your Essay

No essay is complete without quotations. Get in the habit of using quotes to support at least some of the ideas in your essays. Quotes do not need to appear in every paragraph, but often enough so that the essay contains voices aside from your own. When you write, use quotations to accomplish the following:

- provide expert advice that you are not necessarily in the position to know about;
- cite lively or passionate passages;
- include a particularly well-written point that gets to the heart of the matter;
- supply statistics or facts that have been derived from someone's research;
- deliver anecdotes that illustrate the point you are trying to make;
- express first-person testimony.

Problem One
Reread the essays and viewpoints presented in this book and find at least one example of each of the above quotation types.

There are a couple of important things to remember when using quotations:

- Note your sources' qualifications and biases. This way your reader can identify the person you have quoted and can put their words in a context.
- Put any quoted material within proper quotation marks. Failing to attribute quotes to their authors constitutes plagiarism, which is when an author takes someone else's words or ideas and presents them as the author's own. Plagiarism is a very serious infraction and must be avoided at all costs.

Write Your Own Persuasive Five-Paragraph Essay

Using the information in this book, write your own five-paragraph persuasive essay that deals with health care. You can use the resources in this book for information about issues relating to this topic and how to structure this type of essay.

The following steps are suggestions on how to get started.

Step One: Choose your topic.

The first step is to decide on what topic to write your persuasive essay. Is there anything that particularly fascinates you about health care? Is there an aspect of the topic you strongly support or feel strongly against? Is there an issue you feel personally connected to or one that you would like to learn more about? Ask yourself such questions before selecting your essay topic. Refer to Appendix D: Sample Essay Topics if you need help selecting a topic.

Step Two: Write down questions and answers about the topic.

Before you begin writing, you will need to think carefully about what ideas your essay will contain. This is a process known as *brainstorming*. Brainstorming involves asking yourself questions and coming up with ideas to discuss in your essay. Possible questions that will help you with the brainstorming process include:

- Why is this topic important?
- Why should people be interested in this topic?
- How can I make this essay interesting to the reader?
- What question am I going to address in this paragraph or essay?
- What facts, ideas, or quotes can I use to support the answer to my question?

Questions especially for persuasive essays include:

- Is there something I want to convince my reader of?
- Is there a topic I want to advocate in favor of or rally others against?

- Is there enough evidence to support my opinion?
- Do I want to make a call to action—motivate my readers to do something about a particular problem or event?

Step Three: Gather facts, ideas, and anecdotes related to your topic.

This book contains several places to find information about many aspects of health care, including the viewpoints and the appendices. In addition, you may want to research the books, articles, and websites listed in Section Three or do additional research in your local library. You can also conduct interviews if you know someone who has a compelling story that would fit well in your essay.

Step Four: Develop a workable thesis statement.

Use what you have written down in steps two and three to help you articulate the main point or argument you want to make in your essay. It should be expressed in a clear sentence and make an arguable or supportable point.

Example:

Forcing Americans to purchase health insurance is not only unconstitutional it is un-American.

(This could be the thesis statement of a persuasive essay that argues against the part of the Patient Protection and Affordable Health Care Act of 2010 that requires all Americans to be insured by 2014 or pay a fine.)

Step Five: Write an outline or diagram.

a. Write the thesis statement at the top of the outline.

b. Write roman numerals I, II, and III on the left side of the page with letters A, B, and C under each numeral.

c. Next to each roman numeral, write down the best ideas you came up with in step three. These should all directly relate to and support the thesis statement.

d. Next to each letter write down information that supports that particular idea.

Step Six: Write the three supporting paragraphs.

Use your outline to write the three supporting paragraphs. Write down the main idea of each paragraph in sentence form. Do the same thing for the supporting points of information. Each sentence should support the paragraph of the topic. Be sure you have relevant and interesting details, facts, and quotes. Use transition words or phrases when you move from idea to idea to keep the text fluid and smooth. Sometimes, although not always, paragraphs can include a concluding or summary sentence that restates the paragraph's argument.

Step Seven: Write the introduction and conclusion.

See Exercise 3A for information on writing introductions and conclusions.

Step Eight: Read and rewrite.

As you read, check your essay for the following:

- ✔ Does the essay maintain a consistent tone?
- ✔ Do all paragraphs reinforce your general thesis?
- ✔ Do all paragraphs flow from one to the other? Do you need to add transition words or phrases?
- ✔ Have you quoted from reliable, authoritative, and interesting sources?
- ✔ Is there a sense of progression throughout the essay?
- ✔ Does the essay get bogged down in too much detail or irrelevant material?
- ✔ Does your introduction grab the reader's attention?
- ✔ Does your conclusion reflect back on any previously discussed material, or give the essay a sense of closure?
- ✔ Are there any spelling or grammatical errors?

Section Three:
Supporting
Research
Material

Medicare

Facts About Universal Health Care

Editor's Note: These facts can be used in reports to reinforce or add credibility when making important points or claims.

Facts About Health Care in the United States

In September 2010, the US Census Bureau reported that 50.7 million Americans did not have health insurance. This is about 16.7 percent of the total population.

According to data released in June 2010 by the Centers for Disease Control and Prevention:

- 46 million Americans under the age of sixty-five did not have health insurance;
- 40 million Americans eighteen to sixty-five years old did not have health insurance;
- 6.1 million Americans eighteen or younger did not have health insurance;

- 6.9 percent of the population failed to obtain needed medical care due to cost;
- 8.4 percent of Hispanic persons failed to obtain needed medical care due to cost;
- 6.3 percent of non-Hispanic white persons failed to obtain needed medical care due to cost;
- 8.7 percent of non-Hispanic black persons failed to obtain needed medical care due to cost;

- nearly 60 million Americans, or just under one in five people, had been uninsured at some point during the year;
- nearly 33 million people had been uninsured for more than a year;

- the number of children covered by public plans grew from 34.2 percent in 2008 to 37.3 percent in 2009;
- the percentage of adults covered by private plans fell from 68.1 percent in 2008 to 65.8 percent in 2009;
- more than one in five Americans were in a "high deductible health plan." In these, they were responsible for paying at least $1,150 in health costs for an individual and $2,300 for a family before their insurance paid for care.

According to the Kaiser Family Foundation:
- Medicare—a federally funded health insurance program that covers the health care of most individuals sixty-five years of age and over and disabled persons—covered 47.8 million Americans as of September 2010;
- Medicare spending is estimated to account for 12 percent of total federal spending and 23 percent of total national health spending.

Facts About the 2010 Patient Protection and Affordable Care Act

In March 2010, Congress and the Obama administration passed the Patient Protection and Affordable Care Act, which reformed health care in the United States. Some parts of the law are effective as of 2011; others do not take effect until 2012, 2013, or even 2014. The law's key provisions are as follows:
- offers tax credits to small businesses that offer their employees health insurance;
- prohibits health plans from denying coverage to children who have prior health issues, otherwise known as "preexisting conditions";
- prohibits health plans from denying coverage to all people who have preexisting conditions as of 2014;
- prohibits health plans from charging higher premiums based on health status and gender;

- offers Americans who are uninsured because of a preexisting condition access to insurance;
- prohibits insurance companies from dropping people from coverage when they get sick;
- eliminates copayments for preventive services and exempts preventive services from deductibles under the Medicare program;
- requires some health plans to allow young people up to their twenty-sixth birthday to remain on their parents' insurance policy;
- prohibits health insurance companies from placing lifetime caps on coverage;
- requires new private plans to cover preventive services with no copayments and with preventive services being exempt from deductibles;
- ensures that consumers in new plans have access to an effective internal and external appeals process to appeal decisions by their health insurance plan;
- increases funding for community health centers;
- provides funds to increase the number of practicing doctors, nurses, nurse practitioners, and physician assistants;
- requires most individuals to have health insurance as of 2014.

According to CNN.com:
- the act will offer coverage to about 32 million uninsured Americans;
- it will cost $940 billion through 2020 to implement;
- it will reduce the national deficit by $143 billion by 2020.

Americans' Opinions About Health Care

According to a December 2010 ABC News/*Washington Post* poll, of those surveyed:
- 22 percent strongly support the 2010 health care reform law passed by Congress and the Obama Administration;

- 21 percent somewhat support it;
- 14 percent somewhat oppose it;
- 37 percent strongly oppose it;
- 6 percent are unsure;

- 29 percent think the entire 2010 health care reform law should be repealed;
- 30 percent think parts of it should be repealed;
- 38 percent think America should wait and see before deciding;
- 3 percent are unsure.

A November 2010 poll conducted by GfK Roper Public Affairs & Corporate Communications asked respondents whether they thought the changes to the health care system enacted by Congress and the Obama administration in March 2010 will increase the federal budget deficit, decrease the federal budget deficit, or have no effect on the federal budget deficit:
- 57 percent said the changes will increase the deficit;
- 14 percent said the changes will decrease the deficit;
- 20 percent said the changes will have no effect;
- 9 percent were unsure.

For those who said it will increase the deficit:
- 25 percent said the increase will be worth it;
- 72 percent said the increase will not be worth it;
- 3 percent were unsure.

A November 2010 Quinnipiac University poll found the following about Americans' opinions about health care:
- 47 percent think the 2010 health care law should be repealed;
- 30 percent think it should be expanded;
- 18 percent think it should be left as is;
- 6 percent are unsure;

- 85 percent of Republicans think the 2010 health care act should be repealed;

- 5 percent think it should be expanded;
- 5 percent think it should be left as is;
- 5 percent are unsure;

- 14 percent of Democrats think the 2010 health care act should be repealed;
- 53 percent think it should be expanded;
- 28 percent think it should be left as is;
- 5 percent are unsure;

- 48 percent of Independents think the 2010 health care act should be repealed;
- 26 percent think it should be expanded;
- 19 percent think it should be left as is;
- 6 percent are unsure.

According to a *USA Today*/Gallup poll:
- 42 percent of Americans think the 2010 health care law went too far;
- 29 percent think it does not go far enough;
- 20 percent think it is about right;
- 8 percent are unsure.

A November 2010 Kaiser Family Foundation poll asked Americans their opinion on whether they would keep or repeal various elements of the 2010 health care law:
- 78 percent would keep the part of the law that provides tax credits to small businesses that offer coverage to their employees;
- 18 percent would repeal this part;
- 1 percent would keep it but make changes;
- 3 percent are unsure;

- 72 percent would keep the part of the law that gradually closes the Medicare prescription drug coverage gap so seniors will no longer be required to pay the full cost of their medications when they reach the gap;
- 22 percent would repeal this part;

- 1 percent would keep it but make changes;
- 4 percent are unsure;

- 71 percent would keep the part of the law that provides financial help to low- and moderate-income Americans who do not get insurance through their jobs to help them purchase coverage;
- 24 percent would repeal this part;
- 1 percent would keep it but make changes;
- 4 percent are unsure;

- 71 percent would keep the part of the law that prohibits insurance companies from denying coverage because of a person's medical history or health condition;
- 26 percent would repeal this part of the law;
- 1 percent would keep it but make changes;
- 3 percent are unsure;

- 54 percent would keep the part of the law that increases the Medicare payroll tax on earnings for upper-income Americans;
- 39 percent would repeal this part of the law;
- 1 percent would keep it but make changes;
- 6 percent are unsure;

- 27 percent would keep the part of the law that requires nearly all Americans to have health insurance or else pay a fine;
- 68 percent would repeal this part of the law;
- 2 percent would keep it but make changes;
- 3 percent are unsure.

Finding and Using Sources of Information

No matter what type of essay you are writing, it is necessary to find information to support your point of view. You can use sources such as books, magazine articles, newspaper articles, and online articles.

Using Books and Articles

You can find books and articles in a library by using the library's computer or cataloging system. If you are not sure how to use these resources, ask a librarian to help you. You can also use a computer to find many magazine articles and other articles written specifically for the Internet.

You are likely to find a lot more information than you can possibly use in your essay, so your first task is to narrow it down to what is likely to be most usable. Look at book and article titles. Look at book chapter titles, and examine the book's index to see if it contains information on the specific topic you want to write about. (For example, if you want to write about Medicare and you find a book about health insurance, check the chapter titles and index to be sure it contains information about Medicare before you bother to check out the book.)

For a five-paragraph essay, you do not need a great deal of supporting information, so quickly try to narrow down your materials to a few good books and magazine, newspaper, or Internet articles. You do not need dozens. You might even find that one or two good books or articles contain all the information you need.

You probably do not have time to read an entire book, so find the chapters or sections that relate to your topic, and skim these. When you find useful information, copy it onto a note card or into a notebook. You should look for supporting facts, statistics, quotations, and examples.

Using the Internet

When you select your supporting information, it is important that you evaluate its source. This is especially important with information you find on the Internet. Because nearly anyone can put information on the Internet, there is as much false information as true information. Before using Internet information—or any information—try to determine whether the source seems reliable. Is the author or Internet site sponsored by a legitimate organization such as the government? Does the author have any special knowledge or training relating to the topic you are looking up? Does the article give any indication of where its information comes from?

Using Your Supporting Information

When you use supporting information from a book, article, interview, or other source, there are three important things to remember:

1. *Make it clear whether you are using a direct quotation or a paraphrase.* If you copy information directly from your source, you are quoting it. You must put quotation marks around the information, and tell where the information comes from. If you put the information in your own words, you are paraphrasing it.

Here is an example of a using a quotation:

Access to health care is not an American right in the same way that free speech is a right. As the president of the Future for Freedom Foundation points out, "The true nature of rights—the type of rights the Founding Fathers believed in—involved the right of people to pursue such things as health care." (Hornberger) But this is very different than being granted health care outright.

Here is an example of a brief paraphrase of the same passage:

> Access to health care is not an American right in the same way that free speech is a right. The Founding Fathers believed in granting Americans the right to pursue such luxuries as health care—they never intended for the government to provide them outright. Being handed something is very different from being allowed the opportunity to pursue it.

2. *Use the information fairly.* Be careful to use supporting information to say what the author intended it to say. For example, it is unfair to quote an author as saying, "Universal health care is a right" when he or she intended to say, "Universal health care is a right only if gourmet food, three bedroom houses, and other luxuries are to be considered rights—and none of them should be." This is called taking information out of context. It is using supporting evidence unfairly.

3. *Give credit where credit is due.* Giving credit is known as citing. You must use citations when you use someone else's information, but not every piece of supporting information needs a citation.

   - If the supporting information is general knowledge—that is, it can be found in many sources—you do not have to cite your source.
   - If you directly quote a source, you must cite it.
   - If you paraphrase information from a specific source, you must cite it. If you do not use citations where you should, you are *plagiarizing*—or stealing someone else's work.

Citing Your Sources

There are a number of ways to cite your sources. Your teacher will probably want you to do it in one of three ways:

- Informal: As in the example in number I above, tell where you got the information as you present it in the text of your essay.
- Informal list: At the end of your essay, place an unnumbered list of all the sources you used. This tells the reader where, in general, your information came from.
- Formal: Use numbered footnotes or endnotes. Footnotes are placed at the bottom of each page whereas endnotes are generally placed at the end of an article or essay, although they may be placed elsewhere depending on your teacher's requirements.

Works Cited

Hornberger, Jacob G. "Health Care Is Not a Right." Future of Freedom Foundation 1 Jul 2009. < http:// www.fff.org/blog/jghblog2009-07-01.asp > Accessed December 20, 2010.

Using MLA Style to Create a Works Cited List

You will probably need to create a list of works cited for your paper. These include materials that you quoted from, relied heavily on, or consulted to write your paper. There are several different ways to structure these references. The following examples are based on Modern Language Association (MLA) style, one of the major citation styles used by writers.

Book Entries

For most book entries you will need the author's name, the book's title, where it was published, what company published it, and the year it was published. This information is usually found on the inside of the book. Variations on book entries include the following:

A book by a single author:
Jacobs, Thomas A. *Teen Cyberbullying Investigated: Where Do Your Rights End and Consequences Begin?* Minneapolis: Free Spirit, 2010.

Two or more books by the same author:
Pollan, Michael. *In Defense of Food: An Eater's Manifesto.* New York: Penguin, 2009.
——. *The Omnivore's Dilemma.* New York: Penguin, 2006.

A book by two or more authors:
McNerney, Jerry, and Martin Cheek. *Clean Energy Nation: Freeing America from the Tyranny of Fossil Fuels.* New York: AMACOM, 2011.

A book with an editor:

> Friedman, Lauri S., ed. *Introducing Issues with Opposing Viewpoints: Torture.* Detroit: Greenhaven, 2011.

Periodical and Newspaper Entries

Entries for sources found in periodicals and newspapers are cited a bit differently than books. For one, these sources usually have a title and a publication name. They also may have specific dates and page numbers. Unlike book entries, you do not need to list where newspapers or periodicals are published or what company publishes them.

An article from a periodical:

> Burns, William C.G. "Ocean Acidification: A Greater Threat than Global Warming and Overfishing?" *Terrain* Winter/Spring 2008: 169–183.

An unsigned article from a periodical

> "Chinese disease? The Rapid Spread of Syphilis in China." *Global Agenda* 14 Jan. 2007.

An article from a newspaper

> Weiss, Rick. "Can Food from Cloned Animals Be Called Organic?" *Washington Post* 29 Jan. 2008: A06.

Internet Sources

To document a source you found online, try to provide as much information on it as possible, including the author's name, the title of the document, date of publication or of last revision, the URL, and your date of access.

A Web source:

De Seno, Tommy. *"Roe vs. Wade* and the Rights of the Father." The Fox Forum.com 22 Jan. 2009. < http://foxforum.blogs.foxnews. com/2009/01/22/deseno_roe_wade/ > Accessed May 20, 2009.

Your teacher will tell you exactly how information should be cited in your essay. Generally, the very least information needed is the original author's name and the name of the article or other publication.

Be sure you know exactly what information your teacher requires before you start looking for your supporting information so that you know what information to include with your notes.

Sample Essay Topics

Universal Health Care Is a Fundamental Right

Universal Health Care Is Not a Right

Access to Health Care Is a Basic Right

Americans Misunderstand the Concept of Rights in Relation to Health Care

America Has the Best Health Care System in the World

America Does Not Have the Best Health Care System in the World

Socialized Medicine Is Un-American

Socialized Medicine Is Inherently American

Uninsured Americans Threaten the Health Care System

The Problem of Uninsured Americans Has Been Exaggerated

Health Care Spending Is a Serious Problem

The Problem of Health Care Spending Has Been Exaggerated

America's Health Care System Needs to Be Reformed

America's Health Care System Does Not Need to Be Reformed

America Is Experiencing a Health Care Crisis

America's "Health Care Crisis" Has Been Exaggerated

The Government Should Require All Americans to Have Health Insurance

The Government Should Not Require All Americans to Have Health Insurance

Employers Should Be Required to Offer Health Insurance

Employers Should Not Be Required to Offer Health Insurance

Health Care Should Be Driven by Market Forces

Health Care Should Not Be a For-Profit Enterprise

Medicare Should Be Extended to All Americans

Medicare Should Not Be Extended to All Americans

Health Care Should Emphasize Preventative Medicine

Health Care Does Not Need to Emphasize Preventative Medicine

Tax Credits Should Be Used to Improve Access to Health Insurance

Tax Credits Are Not a Good Solution to Problems with the Health Care System

A Public Health Insurance Option Is Good for Health Care

A Public Health Insurance Option Is Not Good for Health Care

All Americans Should Be Offered the Same Health Care Plans as Government Workers

It Is Too Expensive to Offer All Americans Government-Style Health Care Plans

Medicaid Should Be Expanded to Provide Health Care for Families Near the Poverty Line

Medicaid Should Not Be Expanded

The 2010 Patient Protection and Affordable Care Act Will Improve Medical Care

The 2010 Patient Protection and Affordable Care Act Will Not Improve Medical Care

The 2010 Patient Protection and Affordable Care Act Will Worsen Medical Care

The 2010 Patient Protection and Affordable Care Act Did Not Go Far Enough

Smokers Should Pay More for Health Insurance

Smokers Should Not Pay More for Health Insurance

Obese People Should Pay More for Health Insurance

Obese People Should Not Pay More for Health
Insurance

The Military Should Provide Better Health Care for
Veterans

The Military Provides Sufficient Health Care for
Veterans

The Health Care System Is Racist

The Health Care System Is Not Racist

Organizations to Contact

The editor has compiled the following list of organizations concerned with the issues debated in this book. The descriptions are derived from materials provided by the organizations. All have publications or information available for interested readers. The list was compiled on the date of publication of the present volume; the information provided here may change. Be aware that many organizations take several weeks or longer to respond to queries, so allow as much time as possible.

American Enterprise Institute (AEI)
1150 Seventeenth St. NW
Washington, DC 20036
(202) 862-5800 • fax: (202) 862-7177
e-mail: webmaster@aei.org
website: www.aei.org

The American Enterprise Institute for Public Policy Research is a private nonprofit conservative think tank dedicated to research and education on issues of government, politics, economics, and social welfare. AEI opposes top-down health reform that further centralizes power and decision making.

American Hospital Association (AHA)
325 Seventh St. NW
Washington, DC 20004-2802
(202) 638-1100
website: www.aha.org

This is the national organization that represents and serves all types of hospitals, health care networks, and their patients and communities. Close to five thousand hospitals, health care systems, networks, other providers of care and thirty-seven thousand individual members come together to form the AHA.

Association for Healthcare Philanthropy (AHP)
313 Park Ave., Suite 400
Falls Church, VA 22046
(703) 532-6243
website: www.ahp.org

The Association for Healthcare Philanthropy is an international professional organization dedicated exclusively to developing the men and women who encourage charity in North America's health care organizations. Established in 1967, AHP is a key source for education, networking, information, and research in health care philanthropy.

The Brookings Institution
1775 Massachusetts Ave. NW
Washington, DC 20036
(202) 797-6000 • fax: (202) 797-6004
e-mail: brookinfo@brook.edu
website: www.brookings.org

The institution, founded in 1927, is a think tank that conducts research and education in foreign policy, economics, government, the social sciences, and health care–related issues.

CATO Institute
1000 Massachusetts Ave. NW
Washington, DC 20001-5403
(202) 842-0200 • fax: (202) 842-3490
e-mail: cato@cato.org
website: www.cato.org

Founded in 1977, the Cato Institute is a nonpartisan nonprofit libertarian public policy research foundation dedicated to limiting the role of government and protecting individual liberties. Cato supports the position that consumers are better off when they, and not the government, are in charge of how their money is spent. This applies to health care, Social Security, and other areas where the government currently controls the disbursal of tax dollars. Cato supports deregulating the health care industry so that consumers can afford the health care insurance and treatment of their choice.

**The Center for Health Care Policy,
Research and Analysis**
2005 Merrick Rd. #234
Merrick, NY 11566
(800) 442-6177
e-mail: tgarvey@thepolicycenter.org
website: www.healthcarepolicyresearchanalysis.org

The center's mission is to conduct research and analysis toward developing a universal-access health care delivery and single-payer financing system in the United States. In doing so, the center hopes to prevent the premature deaths each year of eighteen thousand uninsured Americans.

Healthcare—Now!
1315 Spruce St.
Philadelphia, PA 19107
(800) 453-1305
e-mail: info@healthcare-now.org
website: www.healthcare-now.org

Healthcare—Now! is an education and advocacy organization that addresses the health insurance crisis in the United States by advocating for the passage of national, single-payer health care legislation. The group's website features compelling patient stories and other information.

Latinos United for Healthcare
2000 L St. NW, Suite 610
Washington, DC 20036
(202) 833-6130
website: http://latinosunitedforhealthcare.org

This group seeks to make health insurance affordable and of higher quality, to end healthcare disparities, and to stop discrimination in care. The group's website features a useful Truths & Myths section, along with an online petition.

National Coalition on Health Care (NCHC)

1120 G St. NW, Suite 810
Washington, DC 20005
(202) 638-7151
website: http://nchc.org

The National Coalition on Health Care is America's oldest, most diverse, and broadest-based organization working to achieve comprehensive health system reform. It is composed of more than eighty member organizations, representing medical societies, business, unions, health care providers, associations of religious congregations, pension and health funds, insurers, and groups representing consumers, patients, women, minorities, and persons with disabilities. It collectively represents more than 50 million Americans. It seeks health care coverage for all, cost management, improvement of health care quality and safety, equitable financing, and simplified administration.

National Committee for Quality Assurance (NCQA)

1100 Thirteenth St. NW, Suite 1000
Washington, DC 20005
(202) 955-3500
website: www.ncqa.org

The National Committee for Quality Assurance is a nonprofit organization dedicated to improving health care quality. Since its founding in 1990, NCQA has been a central figure in driving improvement throughout the health care system, helping to elevate the issue of health care quality to the top of the national agenda. The NCQA seal may be incorporated into a company's advertising and marketing materials only after passing a rigorous, comprehensive review and annually reporting on its performance. For consumers and employers, the seal is a reliable indicator that an organization is well-managed and delivers high-quality care and service.

National Health Care for the Homeless Council
PO Box 60427
Nashville, TN 37206-0427
(615) 226-2292
website: www.nhchc.org

Believing that health care and housing are two fundamental human rights, this organization advocates on behalf of homeless Americans. It advocates for universal health care and for the improvement of current systems intended to serve people who are poor and homeless, researches critical issues, trains and organizes health care providers, and publishes numerous related materials, which are available for download on its website.

Physicians for a National Health Program (PNHP)
29 E. Madison St., Suite 602
Chicago, IL 60602
(312) 782-6006
e-mail: info@pnhp.org
website: www.pnhp.org

PNHP is the only national physician organization in the United States dedicated exclusively to implementing a single-payer national health program. It has more than eighteen thousand members, and it has chapters across the United States. It has advocated for reform in the US health care system since 1987 and lobbied for insurance coverage for the 46 million Americans who have none.

Universal Health Care Action Network (UHCAN)
2800 Euclid Ave. #520
Cleveland, OH 44115-2418
website: www.uhcan.org

UHCAN supports universal health care. To this end, it connects state health care advocacy groups with each other and national organizations to promote the sharing of resources and information, best practices, and collaboration. Interactive maps on its website offer an excellent resource for grasping which health care organizations are active in each state and how to contact state representatives on health care–related matters.

Bibliography

Books

Champy, Jim, and Harry Greenspun, *Reengineering Health Care: A Manifesto for Radically Rethinking Health Care Delivery*. Upper Saddle River, NJ: FT Press, 2010. The authors, pioneers of a methodology called reengineering, apply the process to the health care system.

Christensen, Clayton M., Jerome H. Grossman, and Jason Hwang, *The Innovator's Prescription: A Disruptive Solution for Health Care*. Columbus, OH: McGraw-Hill, 2008. A comprehensive analysis of strategies that promise to improve health care and make it more affordable.

Cohn, Jonathan, *Sick: The Untold Story of America's Health Care Crisis—and the People Who Pay the Price*. New York: HarperPerennial, 2008. Describes how private insurers decide who and what they will cover. Argues in favor of universal coverage with a single-payer system regulated by the government.

Davidson, Stephen, *Still Broken: Understanding the U.S. Health Care System*. Palo Alto, CA: Stanford Business Books, 2010. Offers an explanation of the forces that have caused problems in the health care system. Lays out six elements the author thinks must be included in any plan for change.

Herzlinger, Regina, *Who Killed Health Care? America's $2 Trillion Medical Problem—and the Consumer-Driven Cure*. Columbus, OH: McGraw-Hill, 2007. Exposes the motives and methods of those who have crippled America's health care system. Argues that the current system threatens to erode patient welfare.

Jacobs, Lawrence R., and Theda Skocpol, *Health Care Reform and American Politics: What Everyone Needs to Know*. New York: Oxford University Press, 2010. Explains the 2009 and 2010 effort to reform health care and highlights what the new law offers for average Americans.

Pipes, Sally C., *The Truth About Obamacare*. Washington, DC: Regnery Press, 2010. The author, president of the Pacific Research Institute, argues that Obamacare is even worse than most critics suspect and that the 2010 Patient Protection and Affordable Care Act will make health care more expensive, limit options, lead to deteriorating medical care, and weaken America's already frail economy.

Reid, T.R., *The Healing of America: A Global Quest for Better, Cheaper, and Fairer Health Care*. New York: Penguin, 2009. Argues that all the other industrialized democracies have achieved something the United States has not: providing health care for all citizens at a reasonable cost.

Staff of the *Washington Post, Landmark: The Inside Story of America's New Health Care Law and What It Means for Us All*. New York: PublicAffairs, 2010. This book, by the reporting staff of the *Washington Post*, examines the new health care law's impact on families, doctors, hospitals, health care providers, insurers, and other parts of society.

Periodicals and Internet Sources

Amoroso, Henry J., "Health Care Is a Fundamental Right," *National Catholic Reporter*, September 29, 2009. http://ncronline.org/news/justice/health-care-fundamental-right.

Gawande, Atul, "Getting There from Here," *New Yorker*, January 26, 2009. www.newyorker.com/reporting/2009/01/26/090126fa_fact_gawande?currentPage = all.

Hoven, Randall, "A Conservative Case for Universal Health Coverage," *American Thinker*, December 12, 2007. www.americanthinker.com/2007/12/a_conservative_case_for_univer.html.

Jacoby, Jeff, "What 'Right' to Health Care?," *Boston Globe*, September 13, 2009. www.boston.com/bostonglobe/ editorial_opinion/oped/articles/2009/09/13/what-right-to-health-care/.

Keller, Allen, "Call Health Care What It Is: A Basic Human Right," *Huffington Post*, September 8, 2009. www.huff ingtonpost.com/allen-keller/call-health-care-what-it_b_278765.html.

Kennedy, Ted, "'The Cause of My Life,'" *Newsweek*, July 17, 2009. www.newsweek.com/2009/07/17/the-cause-of-my-life.html.

Lewis, John David, "Health Care, Why Call It a 'Right'?," *Huffington Post*, August 12, 2009. www.huffingtonpost. com/john-david-lewis/why-say-there-is-a-right-b-258188.html.

Los Angeles Times, "The Individual Mandate: It's Constitutional," December 15, 2010. http://articles .latimes.com/2010/dec/15/opinion/la-ed-health-20101215.

Mackey, John, "The Whole Foods Alternative to ObamaCare," *Wall Street Journal*, August 11, 2009. http://online.wsj.com/article/SB10001424052970204 25140457434217007286507 0.html.

McCardle, Megan, "Why I Oppose National Health Care," *Atlantic*, July 28, 2009. www.theatlantic.com/business/ archive/2009/07/why-i-oppose-national-health-care/22300/.

Murray, Iain, and Roger Abbott, "Health Care Is Not a Right," *Washington Examiner*, November 17, 2009. www .washingtonexaminer.com/opinion/blogs/Examiner-Opinion-Zone/Health-Care-is-not-a-right-70302612 .html.

Redmond, Helen, "We Are Not Free: Health Care as a Human Right," *Counterpunch*, February 21, 2008. www .counterpunch.org/redmond02212008.html.

Reich, Robert B., "Why We Need a Public Health-Care Plan," *Wall Street Journal*, June 24, 2009. http://online.wsj.com/article/SB124580516633344953.html.

Sanders, Bernie, "Health Care Is a Right, Not a Privilege," *Huffington Post*, June 8, 2009. www.huffingtonpost.com/rep-bernie-sanders/health-care-is-a-right-no_b_212770.html.

Schwartz, Brian T., "Health Care Is Not a Privilege . . . nor Is It a Right," PajamasMedia, September 8, 2009. http://pajamasmedia.com/blog/health-care-is-not-a-privilege-nor-is-it-a-right/?singlepage = true.

Smith, David, "Healthcare Is NOT a 'Right,'" One NewsNow.com, March 23, 2010. http://www.onenewsnow.com/Perspectives/Default.aspx?id = 948956.

Sullum, Jacob, "There Ain't No Such Thing as a Free Lumpectomy: The Folly of a "Right to Health Care," *Reason*, December 23, 2009. http://reason.com/archives/2009/12/23/there-aint-no-such-thing-as-a.

Towne, Jake, "Health Care Is NOT a Right," Campaign for Liberty, December 23, 2009. www.campaignforliberty.com/article.php?view = 466.

Tucker, William, "Why Healthcare Reform Can't Work," *American Spectator*, March 22, 2010. http://spectator.org/archives/2010/03/22/why-healthcare-reform-cant-wor/1.

Will, George F., "Dr. Leavitt's Scary Diagnosis," *Washington Post*, December 31, 2008. www.washingtonpost.com/wp-dyn/content/article/2008/12/31/AR2008123102778.html.

Worsman, Colette, "Socialized Medicine Will Bankrupt Us," *Concord (NH) Monitor*, May 31, 2009. www.concordmonitor.com/article/socialized-medicine-will-bankrupt-us.

Websites

Change.org's Health Page (http://health.change.org)
This site is run by Change.org, a grassroots social action

platform that partners with Amnesty International, Sierra Club, Human Rights Campaign, and the United Nations Foundation. The site offers breaking news about health care and related topics.

Guaranteed Healthcare.org (www.guaranteedhealth care.org) This site is a project of the California Nurses Association/National Nurses Organizing Committee. It works to expand not only access to health insurance, but access to quality care. In addition to other resources, it features compelling personal stories from Americans who have insurance yet have trouble accessing care.

Health Care for America NOW (http://healthcarefor americanow.org/) This site is run by a national grassroots campaign of more than a thousand organizations in forty-six states representing 30 million people dedicated to winning quality, affordable health care for all Americans. The site makes it easy to understand in what year features of health care legislation kick in based on what current level of coverage a person has; reports and other key documents are available for download on the site.

HealthCare.gov (www.healthcare.gov) This government site is the authoritative source of information for what the health care reform developments mean for all Americans. Multiple articles and a frequently updated health care blog offer current information pertaining to the health care debate.

Health Insurance.org (www.healthinsurance.org) Features useful guides on what health insurance is available by state.

The White House's Health Reform in Action Page (www. whitehouse.gov/healthreform) This page, maintained by the Obama administration, offers Americans up-to-date information on how new health care legislation impacts them. Features a useful interactive map of all fifty states that users can click on to see health care developments in their state.

Index

Gross domestic product (GDP), 33, *34*

Picture Credits

About the Editor

Lauri S. Friedman earned her bachelor's degree in religion and political science from Vassar College in Poughkeepsie, New York. Her studies there focused on political Islam. Friedman has worked as a nonfiction writer, a newspaper journalist, and an editor for more than ten years. She has extensive experience in both academic and professional settings.

Friedman is the founder of LSF Editorial, a writing and editing company in San Diego, California. She has edited and authored numerous publications for Greenhaven Press on controversial social issues such as Islam, genetically modified food, women's rights, school shootings, gay marriage, and Iraq. Every book in the *Writing the Critical Essay* series has been under her direction or editorship, and she has personally written more than twenty titles in the series. She was instrumental in the creation of the series and played a critical role in its conception and development.